A Journey in Traditional Bowhunting

STRONG LEGS

and a

FULL QUIVER

ROBIN L. WEST

Print ISBN: 979-8-35094-195-1

eBook ISBN: 979-8-35094-196-8

Printed in the United States of America

CONTENTS

FOREWORD

"Like arrows in the hand of a warrior, so are the children of one's youth. Happy is the man who has his quiver full of them. . ."

– Psalm 127:4–5

The Bible passage above, attributed to the wisdom of Solomon, speaks to the blessing of having (many) children by comparing them to the feeling an archer might have knowing his quiver was full of arrows before going into battle. Indeed, along with confidence in one's own accuracy and the abilities of the troops by your side, what could be of greater value entering a fight than having sufficient ammunition for what may lie ahead? This book is a story about traditional archery and me. I have been blessed with three children, a loving wife, and many fine friends; freedom in life and great opportunities at work; and enough health and wealth to enjoy a large variety of adventures around the world. Many things have created countless happy memories for me, and many of those have had a common denominator—climbing mountains and hiking long treks with a pair of strong legs, and sneaking through the forest or desert in some wild place with a bow in hand and a quiver full of arrows.

The stories include people and places that are real. I have made every attempt to tell them as I remember them. It is the nature of the game I imagine to focus on successful hunts, but I share too much of some that did not result in the taking of game. Those memories are just as strong and I wouldn't trade them for anything. The book also includes a variety of photographs. They have been taken by me,

1

unless otherwise noted. Many of the pictures depict harvested animals. There was a time that nothing additional would need to be said about such photos—a book about hunting was likely going to show some dead animals. Today, however, some people may anger at the sight of a successful hunter with their prey. I must admit too that I have more feelings for animal welfare than I did decades ago—perhaps from some enhanced maturity produced over time, or maybe a greater sense of the connection between all living things, or even the realization of my own mortality as the years pass. I certainly still hunt animals frequently, kill them occasionally, and eat them happily, but as odd as it may sound, I wish them well—this I define as supporting quality of life in the wild, good habitat, and conservation-minded management; infliction of no unnecessary suffering; and giving a level of respect at all times, including after death. So, while some "grab and grin" photos of harvested animals are included in the stories ahead, I have tried to do so tastefully. I know, however, that some people, who are neither foolish nor ignorant, have developed different values over the course of their lives. I recall a public meeting years ago in Alaska when I was a young wildlife biologist. Wolves on the Kenai Peninsula had been infected by lice (apparently from domestic dogs) and were suffering extreme hair loss. The local state biologist was suggesting that the best course of action might be to try and remove (kill) all the animals in infected packs and maybe stem the problem before it was more widely spread. At the meeting, the biologist held up the tanned skin of a healthy, well-furred wolf alongside one that was missing 30 percent or more of its hair from its back and sides. Local trappers nodded in apparent understanding and agreement; folks from animal rights groups frowned, only seemingly seeing two dead wolves. Diverse thought is a good thing, but if you do not wish to read about hunting or harvest, or see photographs of animals that have met their demise from an arrow, you may not wish to turn the pages further.

Many of the hunting stories are similar to those you might share with a close friend around a campfire, but I do include some tips along the way as well—suggestions that might be called "recipes for success." Instead of any sections being so labeled, however, I chose often to close a chapter with "recipes after success"—this to include a favorite recipe or two for preparing game after a successful hunt. For all the enjoyment that can come from the challenges and rewards of the actual hunt, for me, like for a thousand generations before, the effort is primarily one focused on food. Sure, there are ample grocery stores where I have lived, and easier ways to supply protein for my diet, but there is also satisfaction, and connection to the natural world, when procuring one's own food from nature's bounty.

There are many people who I want to thank for their indirect, but substantial, contributions to this book: Wayne West (my dad) who was not a bowhunter, but a hunter none-the-less and who instilled the love of the outdoors, self-reliance, and a code of ethics; C.R. "Dick" Bonney, a teacher, mentor, and friend; Fred Bear, Jim Brackenbury, Bill Stewart, Tim Meigs, and Allen Boice—bowyers, all now deceased, but whose well-crafted bows I have carried on adventures around the globe; my wife Shannon, for her patience with my obsession; and to the many friends who have helped create these memories. I hope to do them all justice in my story-telling.

Wayne E. West (1935-2008). Photo by Jean Major

C.R. "Dick" Bonney (1929-1999). Photo by Arlene Pleasant

CHAPTER ONE

SMITTEN BY STICK AND STRING

I grew up in rural southwest Oregon in a family that was close to the land—we had irrigated property with a variety of animals, and a large garden and fruit trees. Our primary food for the table, however, came from harvesting deer and elk. My childhood also coincided with a time when "cowboys and Indians" and various adventure series ruled the airways—it was hard to have the old grainy black-and-white TV on for more than a couple of hours without some western airing. I watched many of the programs: *Gunsmoke, Bonanza, Zorro, Big Valley, Daniel Boone, Rawhide, Wagon Train, Have Gun Will Travel, High Chaparral,* and many more. And while the six-gun and carbine ruled on most of the shows, there was an undeniable mystique to the bow and arrow when it appeared, whether in the hands of an Indian warrior, or when used for daring feats by Robin Hood or others.

My first bow was a slender lemonwood stick that pulled about ten pounds. I had discovered it in the attic and asked my dad about it, and he allowed me to use it as I pleased without much discussion or comment. It had a leather boot lace for a string and propelled an arrow only generally toward any intended target. It didn't matter. I carried it everywhere. Even after a tip broke off when it came in contact with the moving spokes of my bicycle, I did not abandon the weapon. I simply shaved off the broken wood so I could affix a crude blade with parachute cord, having a spear, rather than a bow. It probably was more deadly in its new form, but didn't account for any game being procured either, though I did sneak up on a variety of critters and hurl the crude weapon in their general direction a couple of times. Somewhere at about age ten, I was given the standard archery starter kit: a one-piece solid glass twenty-five-pound bow with a molded plastic handle that allowed shooting with either right or left hand. Not knowing a thing about how to use it, I drew the string awkwardly with a nocked arrow between my right thumb and index finger. Pinching and pulling back to release seemed natural, and surprisingly, I became reasonably proficient. It was with this set up I was dropped off one evening by my mom at a local archery club meeting. I was entering middle school and one of the teachers, C.R. "Dick" Bonney, lead a club at the school. Dick lived and breathed archery and passed on his enthusiasm to anyone who demonstrated even a slight bit of interest. I was the ideal student—a virtual sponge, soaking up anything I could learn. That first evening, Dick took my fiberglass bow and restrung it. I had been using it strung backwards for over a year not knowing any better—using it more as a longbow than its intended recurve design. I was embarrassed, but Dick didn't seem to notice or care. He showed me how to draw an arrow properly and line up on the target. At first, I had trouble drawing the bow with my index finger over the nock of the arrow, and middle and ring finger below. Pinching seemed so much more natural and the nocked arrow would often slip away and fall to the ground. But soon I realized I had more control, and strength, with the proper method and again, I felt foolish for my methods, but it did not deter me. I was led to the closest shooting position and quietly and professionally coached. The personal care and instruction made the intimidation and stares of the many other well-equipped and competent archers on the line simply melt away. Magic was created each tine an arrow left the bow and sped toward the target. By the end of the evening, I was hitting the target regularly with a bow and arrows that Dick had loaned me. A few weeks later, a brand new thirty-five-pound Indian Archery recurve arrived. It cost about twenty dollars, and I honestly don't know who paid for it, but I suspect it was Dick. In coming weeks, I would start to compete in mail-in tournaments. By the next year, I was involved in everything "archery" that I encountered: competing in National Field Archery competitions and local shoots as well as being active in Oregon Bowhunters, Siskiyou Bowhunters, and the Rebel Sharpshooters (club at South Junior Highschool in Grants Pass). Over the years, Dick and I shot together, taught together, and hunted together. My father instilled a deep appreciation for hunting, a conservation ethic, a love for animals, and a longing for adventure. Dick gave me archery. The combination took my life to a new level that would shape much of what I would care for and accomplish in life.

Archery became a significant part of the author's life at a young age.

FROM PAPER TO PREY

It is natural I think for a youngster who has been exposed to archery, and who grew up in a family that hunts, to want to try their luck at taking animals with their bow. In some ways, it is a simple adjustment. But in truth, target archery and bowhunting are vastly different endeavors—requiring different equipment and skill sets. There was much to learn. I had already acquired basic outdoor skills, having a father who brought me on his adventures as soon as I was out of diapers, but the archery game was new to him, and I was mostly on my own to learn it. I read everything I could get my hands on, quizzed bowhunters at the local club endlessly, and spent a lot of time using trial and error with different equipment. With a limited budget, I spend hours poring through catalogs before buying anything, often finding what I had purchased didn't work well for me. One of the biggest disappointments I remember was finding that many of the more deadly looking broadheads on the market flew horribly with my arrows, made loud whistling noises, and/or were made from metal so hard that they were difficult to sharpen or so soft that they wouldn't survive more than a few practice shots. I finally discovered *Zwickey* Black Diamond heads and solved the problem for the business end of the arrow for years to come. Dad did help with this part of my learning. He bought me a chainsaw sharpening file and made an antler handle for it and then showed me how to use it. After creating an extended bevel on both sides of the blade, he would use a whetstone and hone the edge razor thin, gently testing it on his wetted arm until it would shave hair. Sharpening a new set of broadheads was slow and tedious for a young boy, but save having access to and skills with a bench grinder, there were no shortcuts. Having razor-sharp broadheads was second in importance only to proper shot placement. Delivering the payload to the target without wobble was also critical and took additional trial and error to get the proper arrow spine and fletching combination. Once mastered, I didn't change the combination for many years.

While deer were the primary target of my early bowhunting efforts, I hunted everything I could. This included mostly small game—rabbits, squirrels, and game birds, as well as carp and bull frogs. I also had a few early opportunities to chase elk, bear, and antelope with my bow. These early big game hunts were generally unsuccessful and humbling. One such hunt was at Gerber Reservoir in southcentral Oregon for pronghorn antelope. In the 1970s, the tags for this "archery only" hunt were by draw only and were always drawable, but few antelope were ever taken. One of the elders from Siskiyou Bowhunters, Floyd Marsh, agreed to help me with the pronghorn challenge, and after a bit of planning, we were off for a week of camping and crawling through volcanic rock and sagebrush. We did see plenty of antelope and got a few shots, but before I continue with that, I want to share a bit about Floyd Marsh. Born in 1907, Floyd had seen a lot of change in his life, but was slow to share his thoughts about most of it—the exception being anything related to archery. He was small in stature and had thick snow-white hair and bushy eyebrows that matched, piercing eyes, and a sly smile. When he spoke it was something that needed to be said and it came out softly and in short sentences. He was a wealth of knowledge of interest to me, having hunted with a bow for over fifty years. He had a beautiful Osage orange recurve with a slender riser that was inlayed with strips of exotic hardwoods, and he shot it well. At the time of his death (in 1982), he was in the midst of forming a new archery club—the Ishi Bowhunters—to celebrate and share traditional bowhunting equipment and techniques and resist the onslaught of technological advances that was rapidly changing the sport. A week hunting with Floyd would prove invaluable to my bowhunting education.

We parked the old Chevrolet sedan under a grove of juniper trees and pitched our tents late in the afternoon of the day preceding the opening of archery antelope season. The car was ill-suited for the rocky two-track roads that accessed the hunting unit, so we would be walking everywhere. We ate sandwiches for dinner and retired to our pup tents early and were up a couple of hours before sunrise the next morning. Floyd wore soft canvas clothing that blended well with the high desert surroundings, but what I noticed most was his footwear. He wore custom moccasins topped with WWI surplus gators. We walked silently in the dark for over an hour and approached an overlook along a brushy rimrock edge as the sun broke over the horizon. Floyd slipped off his pack, leaned his bow against it, and crept to the edge with his binoculars in hand. I followed suit. We sat and glassed for nearly forty minutes before Floyd whispered, "There they are." I moved my binoculars to line up where he was looking and eventually spied a few cream-colored butts that were attached to pronghorn antelope. Excited, I reached for my pack and bow and Floyd grinned. "What's your plan?" he asked. I didn't have one. He said little, and after a few more impatient minutes, I shouldered my daypack and began sneaking toward the distant herd. I looked back once and thought I saw Floyd slip back into the sagebrush and sit down. I continued with my frontal assault but never got closer than 200 yards from the animals. I thought I was invisible to them as I snuck and crawled, but they always seemed to know where I was and continued to keep their distance without ever becoming too alarmed. I met Floyd back at camp after sundown. He inquired softly as we prepared canned stew for dinner, asking how things went. I told him and he smiled, but said little more.

The next few days were largely a repeat of the first. Floyd would find some place to sit, watch, and wait out the day, and I would cover miles of desert—often seeing a fair number of antelope, but never getting close. Finally, the story changed. I spied a lone pronghorn buck on the far horizon feeding slowly toward a ridge that was covered with tall sage and rabbit brush. I ducked down and hurried around to intercept. When I got to the top of the ridge and peered over the bushes, my heart started beating rapidly. The buck was less than seventy yards away and seemingly unaware of my presence. I nocked an arrow and waited. The buck slowly fed toward me. My heart pounded even faster as the buck appeared in front of me, and I drew and released the arrow. It sped toward the animal's chest, and I felt a huge sense of accomplishment only to be quickly deflated. At the last possible moment, the buck hit the deck, flattening himself against the ground, and the arrow slipped harmlessly over his back. He then sped away only to stop and look back my direction at about 120 yards distance, and start feeding again. Apparently, he didn't view me as any significant threat. After retrieving my arrow, I went looking for Floyd. I wanted to tell my story. He had a story of his own. A small herd with a good buck had wandered by his makeshift blind, and he had gotten a good opportunity for a shot only to have his lower bow limb strike some brush when he released his arrow. Like mine, his arrow had also missed an antelope, but it did find a large rock that created a curled broadhead and bent aluminum shaft for a souvenir.

At camp that night, Floyd talked more than he had the entire previous part of the trip, and I listened. He shared that he had many close encounters with antelope in previous days but only the one real opportunity. I had covered a dozen or more miles a day with no more opportunity than him. He had sat in one place, a place that I saw no redeeming value to. There was no water nearby, and it seemingly looked like every other spot in the sprawling desert. He smiled and shared that I may not have seen anything special about the spot, but apparently the antelope did. He confessed that he had seen a great deal of droppings there—both old and new—and that antelope, if undisturbed, for whatever reason, liked to poop in the same general area day after day. With that knowledge, he just looked for a spot that he could be comfortable—avoiding the mid-day sun—and which might allow for a shot opportunity should a buck wander close enough. I'm not sure I ever bought the "poop in the same spot" bit, but I did learn a lot about patience. I didn't have much of it, and it would be something I would need to acquire to increase my likelihood of success.

Floyd Marsh at Gerber Reservoir.

CHAPTER TWO

TRADITIONS AND CHOICES

Traditions are different for different cultures, individual people, and time periods. What is important as a tradition to one person may be nonsensical to another. So too, traditional archery can be defined differently by different people. For most, including references used by state fish and game agencies and regulators, "traditional archery equipment" is generally used to define recurve or longbows—pulled and held with the strength of one's arms without aid of pulleys or cables. Individuals who participate in the sport may go further with their definitions to define traditional archery equipment to include only wooden arrows, fixed blade broadheads, and perhaps only to self-bows (made only with natural materials, without the aid of graphite or fiberglass). Some of this further refinement of the definition may come from personal beliefs, and that is fine, if it is focused on one's self. It can become a distraction, if not a destructive force to the furtherance of the sport, if people allow their traditional beliefs to become too narrow and elitist. I started in the archery world using fiberglass-backed simple recurve bows and longbows, without sights or fancy arrow rests. I never used a release aid and preferred a tab over a glove to protect my fingers. I used wood, fiberglass, and aluminum arrows. I learned with this equipment and shot it endlessly. It was traditional for me.

Fairly soon after I took up the sport of archery, compound bows appeared on the scene. At the time, the choice was primarily between a simple fiberglass set-up marketed by Allen, or a range of strikingly beautiful wooden handled compounds made by Jennings. Within a couple of years, a few other designs hit the market, most notably from Bear Archery, and then the flood gates opened and compound bows (by the mid to late 1970s) were rapidly replacing stick bows. In all fairness, longbows had already largely been replaced by recurves. Until new designs from custom bowyers perfected limb modifications, such as the reflex-deflex design, hand shock from traditional English longbows made them uncomfortable to shoot, and many archers couldn't master the weights needed to accurately propel a heavy hunting arrow with any degree of confidence. I would suggest that most archers at the time gave a compound a try, at least for a while. I was no exception. I got a Bear Polar II compound and used it for a couple of years. I killed a couple of bucks with it too and then gave it to a friend. It was heavy, got tangled in the brush easily, and the deer I killed with it weren't any deader than the ones I had taken with my recurve.

Bear Archery had a marketing scheme in the seventies that proved effective. They sold a lot of archery equipment trying to reach rifle hunters—not necessarily to convert them to archery—but to become "two season hunters." Many states at the time, including my home state of Oregon, had separate archery and rifle seasons for deer and elk, but a hunter wasn't limited in their participation. They could hunt both seasons if they switched weapons. This allowed many people to be in the field for months rather than weeks, allowed using archery equipment early for deer, and the elk rut, and late for elk, and the deer rut, with a rifle in between if desired. What wasn't to like? Two season opportunities, however, faded nearly as fast as they appeared. The longer seasons increased harvest, created crowding in popular areas, and created some worry about potential increased crippling loss from hunters who might be less inclined to learn to shoot their archery equipment well. Bowhunter education started up about the same time that fish and game agencies struggled with dialing back some of the opportunities that they had created. It wasn't long before hunters had to choose their weapon type they would use for a species for the year, at least in many western states. Even that restriction wasn't enough to reduce harvest and crowding over time and many of the historical general hunting seasons went to draw only. Some of this was deemed necessary because of more hunters in the field—the world's population was growing but the world itself wasn't getting any bigger. Some of it too was necessary because of increased success. Hunters armed with compound bows, sights, and release aids generally could learn to shoot reasonably well in less time and could shoot farther and more accurately than those that limited themselves to traditional equipment. Harvest success went up and opportunities had to be reduced.

As people were forced to make choices about how they preferred to hunt, public debate was common. Some rifle hunters wanted less archery opportunity arguing they were inefficient and resulted in unnecessary crippling loss. Counter arguments pointed out that archery equipment had proven effective at taking game for thousands of years and, that used properly, could be a very effective conservation tool. This was argued to be true for specific management goals that benefitted from using short-ranged weapons to reduce game populations in urban areas, to a longer view argument, suggesting that archery seasons allowed more hunters to be in the field enjoying the sport longer and had a valuable place in helping in hunter recruitment and bringing more hunter-conservationists into the fold. These discussions took place at state fish and game regulation meetings, in campgrounds and taverns, and in individual homes, including my own. My Dad was not a fan of bowhunting. He referred to arrows as "wounding sticks" and thought their use should generally be discontinued—artifacts of history and of simpler times. I would argue that the greater the challenge, the greater the reward. He would counter that if I wanted to get really close, I still could, just use restraint with a rifle until I stalked within a few feet and then shoot the animal in the ear. Our discussions were amiable, but he was pretty unchanging, until he saw me kill three bucks in three years. He was at my side with two of the animals, and they both were dead within seconds of being struck by an arrow and were quick and easy to recover. The next season Dad practiced with a Browning recurve and some cedar arrows and went hunting with me. He never shot well and gave it up after the one season, arguing that I was an exception and that most people couldn't shoot well enough to hunt ethically with a bow. It was some years later before I realized that Dad was cross-dominant, and likely why he found trying to shoot a traditional bow instinctively to be very frustrating. Even with his difficulty using a bow personally, and apparent general disapproval of archery seasons, Dad supported my interests. He would drive me to hunting areas, operate a boat so I could shoot carp and bull frogs, and help me when I wanted to make arrows or alternations to my tackle.

Traditional archery tackle was used for a variety of activities.

By the time I had left for college, I had hunted and taken game with shotgun, rifle, handgun, muzzleloader, and both compound and recurve bows. I had a fair degree of competence with all of the weapons, but I already knew my weapon of choice was a traditional bow. The simplicity of design, the growing confidence I had when carrying one, and for numerous reasons that are hard to explain, I was the happiest when carrying a stick bow and a quiver full of arrows. Sometimes I would choose to use a different weapon for a hunt, but in later years, when physical conditions occasionally limited my choice to something other than a traditional bow, I felt a little bit cheated.

GETTING CLOSE

Traditional archery equipment generally does not allow for the same accuracy at distance that using a compound bow with sights offers. Some well-known archers, such as Howard Hill, gained reputations as modern-day Robin Hoods and amazed people with almost mystical abilities using traditional archery equipment, both at targets near and far, but they were the exception rather than the rule. All in all, however, the limited range that the average archer has when choosing traditional equipment, over using more technology, doesn't have to mean much if the archer practices diligently with their equipment, hones their hunting skills to get close to their prey, and uses patience and thoughtful restraint when shooting. Consider in comparison using different firearms during the rifle season. One hunter may choose to carry their grandfather's iron-sighted carbine and be limited in accuracy of approximately fifty yards. Another hunter may buy the latest and greatest flat shooting rifle with bipod and range-finding scope. With practice, they may shoot accurately out to 500 yards or even further. Both are rifles but they do not have the same effective ranges. The same is true with archery equipment. The basic limitations inherent to any particular piece of equipment, individual capabilities, and the amount of practice, will dictate the effective range of an archer. I was lucky. While growing up, I lived in a place that allowed daily practice, and it was rare that I didn't get some in. There were large open fields behind our house, and less than two miles away (an easy bike ride before I drove) was an abandoned archery range. The trails at the old range wound around the mountain to abandoned shooting stations with large cedar bales, some still upright, and others toppled over. It didn't matter. I could roam for hours—shooting from various distances and positions at the abandoned bales. This provided exceedingly valuable practice. An even greater opportunity came with the new range developed on the north side of town. It was too far away to ride my bike, but I frequently bummed rides until I had my driver's license; traveling there then accounted for much of my limited fuel budget. Fortunately, gas was still well under $1.00 a gallon.

Josephine County Sportsman Park was a shooters' dream. It had Olympic-class trap and skeet ranges, large bore and small-bore rifle ranges, a pistol range, and even set-ups for tomahawk throwing competition and training hunting dogs. Most importantly to me, it had three archery ranges. The field target range had classic archery targets set out to eighty yards. The hunter range (to be shot with field points) had circular black and white targets positioned out to seventy yards, and the broadhead range—where broadhead-tipped hunting arrows were shot at various animal cutout targets—had it first shot across a pond at fifty-five yards. As such, I grew used to shooting longer distances. Like others who learned to shoot without the aid of sights, I shot "instinctively." Some would argue that we were "gap shooting" not really shooting instinctively (like being blind-folded and just knowing where to point and release) and this really was just semantics. Instinctive shooter brains, through repetitive trial and error, look for the same sight picture, or gap, between the target and the arrow tip when at full draw. It tells you "instinctively" when to release in order for the arrow to hit where you intend. The further the distance, the larger the gap. The remarkable thing about this is that the formula doesn't change much when using different bows of different draw weights, as long as you adjust the arrow spine and weight accordingly. And for some reason, if you switch to a much heavier arrow, your brain can adjust to the new gap rather quickly with minimal practice. But practice is the key. With the amount of shooting that I was doing, I became deadly at fifty to fifty-five yards, hitting the kill zone 95 percent of the time or more. At sixty yards, I was only about 30 percent effective. At seventy, less than 20 percent, and at eighty, well, that was only one shot on a walk-up target to start the field archery round, and if I hit the mark, it was cause for celebration. It didn't happen very often. Everyone should know their limitations and keep their shots within their effective range. I knew mine well. As the years passed, my effective range dropped to forty to forty-five yards and then thirty to thirty-five and continues to decline. This is largely due to aging shoulders and the inability to shoot with the repetition I once did. I have accepted this somewhat graciously and adapted my hunting strategies accordingly.

* * *

It is fun to retell stories of long and successful shots, and I will share a couple, but first, it is important to emphasize that a good and ethical bowhunter does not exceed their known effective range just because it is the best opportunity that they are likely to get or they otherwise conclude it "is now or never." I tried to emphasize when teaching bowhunter education that every time a hunter draws and releases an arrow at an animal, they should be 100 percent certain they are going to kill it. They may not of course, but that should be the standard for whether they take the shot or not.

The very longest shot I ever took at an animal, and killed, was a snipe on the wing at approximately seventy-two yards. Now folks who know that the common snipe is not a mystical creature that you trick someone into "hunting" also know that it is an extremely small creature that flies in rapid and erratic patterns. As such, the thought of taking one on the wing with bow and arrow at any distance, let alone over seventy yards, is somewhat laughable. I am reminded however, of an old saying that my dad was fond of, "Even a blind hog finds an acorn sometimes." Snipe were abundant in the wet fields and irrigation ditches that surrounded our property. I hunted them often. Their season overlapped with a generous waterfowl season, but ducks rarely wandered into the area, so I focused on what was there. Dozens of stalks resulted in no shots, and most shots resulted in misses. I also rarely even tried to shoot the birds on the wing. My strategy was to flush a bird, watch it zip around and land somewhere ahead on the muddy banks of a ditch, let it settle a bit, and then creep up to the area and try and spot the bird through the grass before it spotted me. At that point, I would attempt a shot, if I had been stealthy enough. Suffice it to say that I never hurt the snipe population very much. I killed three or four over the years on the ground, and one day, a bird flushed beneath my feet and flew directly away up the main irrigation ditch channel. I drew and released a flu flu and struck the flying bird in the middle of its long bill, breaking its neck and killing it instantly. That day, I was the blind hog.

And then there was the longest shot that I didn't make. I didn't miss either. . . Belding's ground squirrels, also referred to as "sage rats" were deemed to be pests and were abundant throughout much of eastern Oregon in the spring. Some archery clubs would hold competitive hunts/shoots to correspond with the squirrels' emergence and bowhunters far and wide would come for a camping trip, catch up with old friends, and the opportunity to chase the abundant squirrels. I never participated in any of the organized events, but I did chase the squirrels whenever the opportunity arose. On one such spring outing, I was wandering about looking for ground squirrels near Baker, Oregon. I was accompanied by Kevin Bennett, a fellow "sleeper" which referred to our status as volunteer firefighters whom lived in the fire station in LaGrande while attending nearby Eastern Oregon State University. Now Kevin was a practical joker and always had a twinkle in his eye. His favorite "gotcha" involved him wearing a monkey mask and using the antiquated fire pole system to travel around the old fire station and sneak up behind people and grab them and yell. It was lots of fun for Kevin, but not so much for everyone else. It was with this history of practical jokes that preceded Kevin and me chasing sage rats with bows and arrows. We had shot a few, but mostly were just walking around enjoying the spring sunshine. I saw a squirrel creep out of its hole, and I drew back and pinned it to the ground. I looked over and Kevin hadn't noticed, so I kept quiet. As we worked our way around the end of a reservoir, I stopped and looked back to where we had come and drew an arrow from my back quiver, pulled back, elevated greatly, and released a high arching shot that sailed across the water and landed approximately 200 yards away. Kevin stared at me but said nothing. I shot a few more times before he asked what I was doing. I said that I was shooting at a squirrel, but I had got him so was done. He laughed questioning and let out, "Yeah, sure" and followed me back around the reservoir to where a handful of arrows had rained down—one being in the middle of a very dead ground squirrel. I never told him the kill shot had been about 20 feet vs 200 yards, but I smiled when I thought about it and silently whispered, "Take that monkey man"! Kevin still has a great sense of humor and hopefully will retain it if he ever reads this story.

Kevin Bennett at LaGrande Fire Department.

CHAPTER THREE

ALASKA ADVENTURES

I was fortunate to get work in Alaska within months of graduating from college. Armed with a new wildlife management degree and a lot of youthful energy, I traveled north to Anchorage with a one-way ticket and six pieces of luggage in late October 1978. Nights were much longer already at that time of year, compared to Oregon, and snow was already accumulating deeply in what would turn into a very snowy winter. None of this might have mattered too much except I didn't have a car, or enough money to buy one, and I had to walk to work to the U.S. Fish and Wildlife Service office from wherever I could find to live with my extremely limited budget. I walked nearly an hour each way to work, mostly in the dark, and often post-holing in drifted snow to avoid getting hit by passing cars. Gradually I settled in, bought an old beater pick-up and started exploring the country.

Alaska in the late 1970s was booming. The pipeline was pumping oil, and the economy was strong. Less than a million people lived in an area 20 percent the size of the rest of the United States and hunting and fishing opportunities were abundant. A resident could buy an annual license to hunt, fish, and trap for under fifty dollars and most tags were free. You could take one Dall ram, one mountain goat, up to seven deer of either sex, five or more caribou, three black bear, a moose, and one grizzly/brown bear (for twenty-five dollars); plus a bison and muskox if you were lucky enough to draw a permit. Seasons were long and game was plentiful. All the new opportunities were special—part of a dream come true after years of digesting everything I could read about Alaska in *Outdoor Life* and *Field and Stream* magazines. Still, I didn't have a lot of money so charter trips to the bush were few, and I tried to maximize my success when I planned my trips afield. I generally chose to leave my bow at home for the first few years, opting instead to increase the likelihood of bagging game.

I'm reminded of the Dustin Hoffman movie, *Little Big Man*, where he retold his adventures in the West during the late 1800s. He shared about being a mule skinner for Custer at the Battle of Little Bighorn, and many other stories that he described as phases in his life, like his "gunfighter phase." As a young single wildlife biologist in Alaska, I went through a lot of phases: deckhand on a commercial halibut boat, trapper, and handgun hunter. At some point fairly early on, I decided that I wasn't ready to stick primarily with archery equipment for my outings, but I still desired a short-range weapon that compromised on challenge and success. Hunting handguns were relatively light and easy to pack, were lethal if kept to acceptable range, and provided at least a little defense against an unfriendly bear. I used a variety of handguns, from the Thompson Contender chambered for 30–30 or 45–70, to the Colt Delta Elite in 10 mm. For the most part however, I stuck with a stainless-steel Ruger Redhawk or Super Blackhawk, both chambered for .44 magnum. While times have changed, in those days finding quality factory loads for handgun hunting was a challenge, so I loaded my own. I developed a load for my 44s that included a well-built 300-grain soft point bullet that was backed by as much slow burning powder that I could cram safely into the case. When I set and crimped the bullets, they were indented on their lead points with the shape of the inside of the die.

There was no airspace left between the primer and bullet. The rounds were "hot" but safe in the Ruger revolvers and extremely accurate as well as lethal. With them I killed sheep, goats, deer, black bear, caribou, and one grizzly bear. Many of the animals dropped where they stood, and none went very far after being struck. The secret to my success wasn't so much the load and bullet that I was using as much as where I placed it. I practiced a lot—at least fifty rounds a week on average. I practiced out to 100 yards but rarely fired at an animal over forty.

Author during his Alaska "handgun phase".

After a few years of hunting almost exclusively with a handgun in Alaska, I got the urge to pick up a bow again. I was surprised how quickly it came back to me. The years of instinctive shooting were imprinted in my brain, much like riding a bicycle. The hardest part was gaining strength to pull bows suitable for hunting Alaska game. I had cut my teeth on shooting bows in the forty- to fifty-pound class, and technically they were legal in Alaska for larger animals, but I felt sixty-pounds was better and that is what I worked into, ultimately using sixty- to sixty-five-pound bows for most of my Alaska hunting.

My first serious Alaska bowhunting efforts focused on Sitka blacktail deer on Kodiak Island. The season was long (over four months) and the bag limit generous (seven deer of either sex). More importantly, however, the animals were abundant, tasty, and seemingly made for bowhunting. Hunters who have pursued whitetail deer might think Sitka blacktails are dumb when first encountering them. The truth is that they are just different. The blacktails on Kodiak have no real natural predator, save the giant brown bears that call the island home, and the bruins are far more proficient at catching salmon than deer and probably take very few. The island terrain has lots of cover and relief and the deer are quite stalkable. Too, they will often come to a fawn bleat call (but so will bears). In my first hunt to Kodiak, I killed four bucks with four arrows in four days. Hunting Kodiak made me a better hunter. In coming years, I can credit Kodiak deer hunting experiences with increasing my overall skills in stalking, timing my shot, and trailing game.

The best time to hunt Kodiak for deer is during the rut in mid- to late November. Some disadvantages to this timing exist however: the days are short and so tent time is long, the weather can be nasty, and some freshwater lakes freeze, limiting floatplane access to saltwater. Some of the seasonal impacts can be mitigated by finding a cabin to use, but most that are available to rent are also popular with others, so the hunting will not as likely be as good as it would be if chartering a float plane to an undeveloped remote site. Though expensive, the best of both worlds can be achieved by chartering a fishing boat that can access far away bays, put you ashore during the day, give you a cozy place to sleep at night, and feed you very well to boot.

I mentioned Kodiak bears in passing, but they deserve a little more attention. While I only know of one hunter in modern times killed there (after taking a deer), encounters are frequent and should be near the top of the list when thinking about how to plan and undertake a Kodiak hunt. Know that the bears can be out and about even in winter and that they can smell a gut pile or deer meat for miles away. Combine that with trees to hang meat being scarce, particularly on the south end of the island, special consideration is warranted for handling harvested venison. I suggest using a portable electric fence around your tent, but don't expect one to deter a bear from meat. If you can hang the meat high off the ground, you of course should, or put it inside a separate building if in a camp with hard-sided structures. Alternatively, I have found that you can bone and cool the meat and put it in a clean meat bag, place it a double layer of garbage bags (with the air removed), and then in a well-made float bag. You then submerge it in a lake. This eliminates almost all smell and the results are similar to putting the meat in a refrigerator. Finally, I recommend bringing both bear spray and a good firearm— "good" being a general term for something big enough to stop a brown bear, if need be, and one in which you have both confidence and competence. No one should want to shoot a bear with a gun on a bow hunt for deer, and with reasonable precautions, it is exceedingly unlikely that you would have to do so, but you should be prepared nonetheless. I usually keep a .12-gauge shotgun with both slugs and rubber bullets in camp, and carry both bear spray and a .44-magnum revolver when hunting. I also have enough experience with both bears and handguns to know that my choices could be minimally effective in many situations. Finally, I have all but given up calling. I have killed many deer at close range with a bow using this method, but I have also had one too many chilling experiences with large brown bears stalking me, even after I stopped calling, yelled and waved my arms, dropped my bow and drew my handgun. At such times, the .44 seemed exceedingly small.

Kodiak Island Sitka blacktail.

* * *

Planning an Alaskan hunting trip requires considerable thought regarding contingencies. Taking care of harvested meat, and preventing unwanted bear encounters, are major considerations, but generally topping the list in planning are the overall transportation and logistics variables and the uncertainty of the weather. Most Alaska hunting includes transportation to remote locations via small plane, boat, or ATV. Much also includes chartering—where you depend on someone else to drop you off and come and get you. Their timeliness depends on a whole host of things: getting backed up on their schedule and having to transport others before you, health or mechanical issues, and the weather. On one hand the weather is not something you can plan on—but on the other, it is something you should definitely plan for. Delays in charters are extremely common and having an extra week of supplies over what you think you might need is always a good idea when left in some distant place. Today's satellite communication devices have changed the game somewhat. I can't count the number of times I had camp broke, waiting an early morning pick up, only to put the tent back up when the charter didn't show and nightfall was approaching. Nowadays, the chances of not being picked up on time have not lessened, but you might be able to know about delays with more certainty. And while weather events can prove inconvenient to travel, they are equally important in planning for your time camping and hunting. What you have with you when the bush plane becomes small over the horizon, is all you will have until it reappears. There are no stores to visit at the end of a day's hunt. Weight will be limited, so just taking lots of stuff isn't the answer—taking the right stuff is. Special considerations should be given to a quality tent and sleeping bag, raingear, food, fuel, and the like. How you store and cook your food to reduce issues with bears is important. Being ready to keep meat for an extended period is also critical, along with dealing with abundant biting insects (mosquitos, flies, and/or gnats, depending on the time of year). Also important is having sufficient batteries for communications and other equipment and planning on how to transport restricted items (such as bear spray, strike anywhere matches, lighters, propane cannisters, etc.). Finally, your clothing must allow you to be comfortable in a variety of weather conditions and also use your bow effectively. I have taken Alaskan game in temperatures as warm as nearly 80 degrees and as cold as 26 degrees below zero. Shooting a bow in cold weather could mean dealing with a potentially puffy parka and heavy mittens—neither conducive to effectively drawing your bow and releasing an arrow. I choose to dress in tight layers and use an extra-long armguard (so my string doesn't strike clothing upon my release) and to have tight glove liners and a shooting tab under heavy mittens (which I remove right before a shot). Whatever clothing one chooses, it is important to practice with the set up before actually hunting in it. This means everything, including broadbrim hats (which can impede full draw), raingear (which can be too stiff to achieve full draw), and even hip boots (which can make shooting from a kneeling position a little different).

*Hunting in Alaska can entail weather extremes;
this moose was taken at twenty-six degrees below zero.*

* * *

Caribou are an iconic Alaskan animal that are abundant and extremely fun to hunt with a bow. Their numbers fluctuate, and some biologists believe that over time the species may not fare well with changes in climate patterns in the north, but when I lived in the interior and western Alaska, they were a food staple for me, and I hunted them more than any other Alaskan game.

There are some plusses and minuses when pursuing caribou. On the plus side, they can be easy to find as they generally inhabit open tundra. On the negative side, they can be difficult to get within bow range of because they generally inhabit open tundra. Other plusses include the species can be curious, may not go tremendous distances when spooked, and are not particularly tenacious to life (generally don't go far after being hit). These generalizations are in comparison, say to elk. Other negatives include that the animals are frequently in herds (with lots of eyes, ears, and noses working) and are often on the move. I mention this last point as I have had multiple opportunities at caribou moving by me while I kept crouched in a low stationary position, well within range, only not to get a shot at an un-spooked animal because I couldn't lead them enough, quickly enough. Earlier season hunting can help with this problem—often single bulls may be found in late summer and early fall, bedded in low willow patches or feeding in relatively small areas with another bull or two. This changes during migration and during the rut when hunters should expect caribou to slowly but surely cover tons of ground. This is apparently an ancient herd strategy where thousands of animals seek to make a living over the same land year after year.

Caribou offer a fairly large kill target area but hunters still will do best if they can shoot well to at least forty yards. This can push the limits for traditional archers, and to complicate things, kneeling shots are most likely, so lots of practice at longer distances and from low crouched positions will help immeasurably. Caribou are significantly larger than deer so a good pack frame is needed for hauling meat. I like to bone mine in the field so I am not packing anything I don't want to keep later, but hunters need to check the regulations for the area they are hunting as in some cases it is required to leave the bones in the quarters. The rule is meant to address potential wanton waste of meat, but it has its own problems. Extra weight can mean extra trips packing, and increase the odds of bears or wolves helping themselves in the meantime, as well as potential extra cost to fly out the meat, particularly if you have multiple animals. No matter. The rules are the rules and they change from time to time so hunters should check the latest regulations for the area they intend to hunt before going. Additionally, in all areas in Alaska, it is illegal to pack out the trophy portion of the animal, including horns or antlers, before all edible meat has been removed from the field (although they can be included along with meat in the last load). Some final thoughts about hunting caribou, and hunting in Alaska in general. A nonresident cannot legally hunt without a guide (or close relative who is a resident) for Dall sheep, mountain goats, or grizzly (brown) bears, but they can for other species. Black bear and deer are the easiest hunts for nonresidents to undertake by themselves without much assistance. Caribou can be relatively easy too but often require a bit more logistics planning and specialty gear. Moose are the hardest for nonresidents to tackle without help given their sheer size and the remoteness of where most trophy bulls are taken. Give serious thought to all aspects of a moose hunt before undertaking one. Hunting them can be one of the most rewarding experiences that a hunter will ever have, or one of the worst. Finally, Alaska has a unique rule that allows a hunter to use their tag on the species it was purchased for, or any other species of equal or lesser value that has an open season. This means someone that buys a caribou tag could use it to tag a deer or black bear instead. Because of overlapping seasons and unpredictable opportunities, it can make sense for a nonresident hunter to buy a moose tag even if they are primarily expecting to encounter caribou, if they have any interest in tagging a moose on their caribou hunt. Of course, they could also buy both tags to begin with.

Caribou were a primary food source.

RECIPES AFTER SUCCESS

All Alaska game that I have eaten has been good; however, everyone has their preferences. Mine start with bison (of which I only got one while in Alaska), then goat (for basic flavor and marbling of fat), followed by moose, sheep, caribou, and bear. When the kids were all at home, my family would generally eat the equivalent of one moose, two caribou, or four deer per year. Caribou was the most common meat in our freezer, and though I listed it lower on the list of my favorites compared to other game, it still is very good. The only exception to this is if a large bull is taken in the rut (usually October). They have long hair and a striking white mane that time of year—making wonderful trophies—but the meat quality can suffer. It truly is the only big game animal that I think the rut can make a substantial difference in meat quality. It may take on a musky scent that permeates the kitchen and leaves guests not asking for seconds. If you avoid old bulls in the rut, I think you will be more than happy with caribou meat and you can use it like any other red meat in any number of recipes. Here's one for caribou kabobs.

Take about two pounds of a good cut of meat (from rump or backstrap) and cut into cubes of about an inch or a little more. Cover and marinate in Italian salad dressing for two to three hours at room temperature. Salt to taste and grill until meat is rare to medium rare (usually about eight to ten minutes depending on the grill's temperature). Place meat on skewers, careful not to burn yourself, alternating mushrooms, peppers, onions, and cherry tomatoes if you like, and grill another eight to ten minutes.

CHAPTER FOUR

A SNAKE IN THE GRASS

I grew up intrigued with nature and all wild animals. That, combined with my interest in hunting and fishing, led me to choose a career in wildlife management. Admittedly though, I didn't view all animals equally. I loved the playful nature of river otters, the amazing hovering flight of hummingbirds, and the inherent beauty of a drake wood duck or harlequin duck. I found pleasure when I heard a bull elk bugle close by or saw a cutthroat trout rise to take a fly. I loved watching a beaver work to plug a hole in its dam in the fading light of day or a wren busily bring twigs to its nest as the sun first warmed the morning. But I didn't like snakes. I can't say I hated them, or was deathly afraid of them, but I didn't like them nonetheless, and as a youth I sometimes killed them for no good reason. Perhaps I learned this from my dog Cookie, a small half beagle and half dachshund. She would grab every snake she could catch and shake it so fiercely that it died near instantly. They were mostly harmless garter snakes that foolishly entered our fenced yard. Some of my feelings toward snakes could also be from an early experience I had handling one. It didn't take kindly to my grasp and latched onto the web of flesh between a thumb and forefinger with a vice-like grip and wouldn't let go. When I finally did pry it off, it left a u-shaped indentation that didn't even break the skin, but creeped me out nonetheless. And then there was my first experience with a rattlesnake. I was helping a teenaged friend, Doug Estes—a fellow "arrow flinger"—on an antelope hunt. He had drawn a tag in eastern Oregon and Dad had driven us over and camped with us while Doug and I tramped around the desert in search of pronghorn. We had brought our bows and did some small game hunting with them during pre-season scouting, but Doug decided to use his grandfather's .308 for the actual pursuit of pronghorn. It was the middle of opening day, and we were traveling fast across open country scanning far ahead, looking for any sign of antelope, when suddenly something hit my right leg just at the top of my boot. I looked down and was shocked to see a rattlesnake hanging onto my leg—its fangs tangled into my blue jeans. I shot my leg up in a violent kick and the snake detached and hit the ground, immediately coiling and striking back toward me. While it hadn't rattled before the first strike, it did then—a lot! I grabbed Doug's rifle and dispatched the creature. This started a long tradition of me killing poisonous snakes upon encountering them. A tradition that I did eventually outgrow. For many years now, I have adopted a live and let live attitude toward snakes, poisonous or not. The exception is when they would hang out close to the house when we lived in southwestern Oregon after retirement. Having a wife working in the thickets of her flower garden, and a near blind German wirehaired pointer that thought lizards were toys, influenced me to remove rattlesnakes that took up residence near the yard. One such instance reminded me too why I still don't really care for the critters. I took the head off a large rattlesnake that was living in a hole by our car. Though headless, it continued to rattle, coil, and strike out full length, only to repeat the activity for what seemed like a gruesomely long time. That image is forever imprinted in my mind and so I have to admit that I continue to have a thing about snakes.

I imagine no one can spend years traveling around the globe in pursuit of game and adventure without a few stories about encounters with snakes. The following are a few of mine. The first two are work stories as they, along with the experiences shared above, help explain my evolution of thought on the matter of serpents. The remaining stories then are from bowhunting adventures in the United States and Africa. The memories are just as strong as when taking game with a bow—perhaps stronger.

TRAPPING WOOD RATS

My first paying job after graduating from Oregon State University was to work as a mammologist with an interdisciplinary team studying riparian habitats in the Warner Valley of southcentral Oregon. It was a summer job only, financed by a National Science Foundation grant, and my job was to estimate the abundance and diversity of mammals, reptiles, and amphibians associated with the varied stream; hot springs; alkali lake, marsh, and playa habitats in the area. Other fledging scientists were looking at birds, plants, or insects in the same locations. While my task was overly broad, the real focus was on small mammals, of which there were many varieties, including mice, squirrels, kangaroo rats, rabbits, chipmunks, and others. The primary method of determining what was present, and estimating abundance, was intensive live-trapping on large grids. Assisted by Pat Matthews (who also joined me for a break at the end of the summer for a mule deer bow hunt on nearby Hart Mountain), we would set out a hundred or more baited traps and return early the next morning to check them. The majority of the traps used were Sherman live traps—small collapsible aluminum devices that had a trigger plate toward the back that, when depressed by an animal entering, would immediately release the spring-loaded door and trap the animal inside. The grids would be trapped for multiple nights as estimating population size required mark-recapture procedures. And of course, there were field notebook pages to fill out: date, time, location, air temperature, species, sex, weight, and unique markers (to identify the animal upon recapture). As we approached a trap that had been triggered, we would pull out the notebook and get ready to record information and then push the trap door open ever so slightly to peer in and determine what the species was—to start filling in the blanks in the notebook before actually removing and handling the animal. Hefting a closed trap often gave some idea of its contents. If it was light, frequently, it would be a deer mouse or canyon mouse; if it was of medium weight, perhaps a kangaroo rat or chipmunk; heavier still, likely a ground squirrel or wood rat. The heaviest was an occasional pygmy cottontail rabbit that somehow managed to cram its entire body in the trap before the hinged door snapped shut. That is what I thought I had upon picking up a particularly heavy closed trap one morning. Imagine my surprise, when I pushed the trap door open slightly to view its contents only to have a large flat and scaly triangular head appear, followed by a few rapid tongue flicks in my direction. I was so shocked, I dropped the trap and upon hitting the ground it broke open and the rattlesnake slithered away between my feet, disappearing into some adjacent rabbit brush. It wasn't to be my last experience with learning the ways of the wily serpent that summer however. Several times, I would walk in the high desert in the heat of the day and spot a rattlesnake at shoulder height, or eye level, draped loosely across branches of greasewood or tall sage. While they couldn't easily strike from such a perch, and were probably just casually hunting small birds or seeking relief from the scorched ground on a hot summer day, the experiences really creeped me out too! Snakes are supposed to be on the ground, aren't they?

Rattlesnake kept at arm's length – Warner Valley, Oregon.

MISSISSIPPI SWAMPS

My first permanent job with the U.S. Fish and Wildlife Service was as a wildlife technician working at Hillside National Wildlife Refuge Complex out of Yazoo City, Mississippi. For a westerner, there was much new about the place, and I found most of it extremely exciting. There were long deer hunting seasons—both for bow and gun— and at the time, the bag limit was one deer a day. The waterfowl and turkey hunting were superb, and I still remember everything good about spectacular days of fishing for bass and catfish that ended with a tasty fish fry under a star-lit sky. But one of the new things I didn't care so much for was the snakes. They were often of the poisonous variety (rattlesnakes, copperheads, and water moccasins), abundant, and sneaky. They didn't play by the rules. Just like the rattlesnakes in southcentral Oregon not knowing they weren't supposed to be in the bushes high off the ground, the snakes down south didn't know they were supposed to swim on top of the water, where you could see them coming. The water in Oregon was generally clear, and every snake I saw there (whether a garter, gopher, or rattlesnake) swam on top of the water. I found in Mississippi the water to generally be muddy, and that many of the snake species, most notably the water moccasin (or cottonmouth), would slip beneath the water like a submarine and reappear somewhere least expected. This made for interesting times while wading through dark cypress swamps setting up wood duck nest boxes or when paddling a canoe around at night with a spotlight to survey alligators. You might hear a slight splash as a snake on a limb somewhere ahead relaxed at your approach. You then would wonder what species it was, and where it was. Sometimes when these things were going through your mind something would suddenly brush against your leg in the murky water below—most probably a catfish or gar, but you never really knew. These fears were fueled by an oft told tale at the time of a local fishermen who was wading the cypress swamps when a water moccasin dropped out of a tree into the small gap between the angler's chest waders and chest, biting him repeatedly and resulting in his death. A fluke for sure, but the image was a bit haunting.

Once, fellow technician Shaw Davis and I were working to control nutria. The exotic rodents reproduced rapidly and were a constant threat to the many dikes and levees needed to hold water on the refuge. I was ashore shooting with a .22 rifle, while Shaw was wading around picking up the animals I had shot. Someone at Mississippi State University was doing a study on the species, and we would save as many as we could. Shaw was sliding around in pretty deep water, close to the top of his chest waders, and picking up as many animals as he could hold before slogging slowly back to shore to deposit the carcasses on the bank. He had several, half dragging and floating them along, as he stooped slightly to pick up another. All of a sudden, he leapt back and shouted, "Water moccasin!" having mistaken the scaley dark tail of a snake for a similar looking deceased nutria tail. Apparently too, the critter didn't really want to be picked up and shipped off to the University. No harm was done beyond a little splash over the waders and a decision to abandon the work for the day.

Urban legend and campfire stories about snakes may share such things as the practice of sleeping with a horsehair lariat around your bedroll if you lay on open ground at night in snake country—supposedly if they were attracted to your body heat, they would also be deterred from getting too close if attempting to slither over the bristly rope. I don't know if the practice works, and probably never will, as I generally opt to enclose myself in a tent, or at least a bivy bag that has a floor and zipper. Another such legend, however, I think may have some potential truth. It goes something like, "Don't be the third person hiking in snake country—the first will wake 'em up, the second, will make 'em mad, and the third will get bit." I just so happened to be the third person one day when hiking out of a Mississippi swamp after assisting with survey work on some new refuge land. The surveyor, an older gentleman from the regional office, led the way, carrying only a satchel. Shaw followed toting a transit and some other equipment, and I brought up the rear, heavily laden with a large tripod and some boundary stakes. I saw something move at my feet and an extremely large and agitated water moccasin coiled and struck out at me as I lurched backward. It repeated the strike as it chased me on my retreat. Having dropped my load, I drew an old Smith and Wesson Model 10 revolver that was loaded with number nine shot, and fired. The blast stopped the attack. In all my encounters with snakes over the years, aggressive or otherwise, that was the only one I really felt I needed to destroy to protect myself. At least that is what I thought at the time.

Water moccasins may conceal themselves, or become aggressive.

OUT OF AFRICA

Much of the hunting in Africa occurs during the dryer and colder months—June through October—which coincides with winter and spring there. As such, snakes can be dormant that time of year. I do want to emphasize CAN be. My wife Shannon joined me on my first bowhunting safari and spent the first few days in a blind with me—from before daylight until dusk. The first two days we were in elevated thatched stands near water. We saw plenty of game and took many pictures, but didn't release an arrow. Either the game encountered was not on my list of species I was interested in (or could afford) or they did not present an acceptable shot opportunity. On the third day, we were in a pit blind dug into the ground. It was situated in a small pass between a dense thicket and a rocky bluff—creating a natural pinch point for animals moving through the area. Like on the first two days, many animals passed by and it was wonderful because it was all new to us. We soaked up every sight, sound, and smell of the African veld. In mid-day, we were listening to a covey of francolin move nosily through the dry leaves immediately outside the blind. They made kind of a "scritch, scritch, scritch" noise as they slowly progressed. After a spell, the noise changed to more of a "shliiish, schliiish, schliiish," and I slowly pushed aside the burlap flap draped over the entrance to the blind and peered out. There I discovered a rather large snake moving towards the entryway. I shared my discovery with my wife who laughed and assumed I was joking. I assured her I wasn't. There were two shooting windows, but they were too small to crawl out. The only exit was the same way we had entered, and that was now blocked by a creature which seemed to really want to come in for a visit. I looked at my bow and grimaced at the thought of using it to dissuade the serpent from entering. It was a custom recurve, and the snake was large and the ground was rocky. Instead, I grabbed a case that held some spare arrows—a Cabela's fishing rod case that was covered in a rough canvas fabric. I used it to push the snake back from the entryway, but each time I did it would coil and lunge forward, hitting the case and catch its fangs in the fabric. I would shake it loose, and then we repeated the joust for a few more times before the critter finally decided it would go elsewhere for its siesta. Needless to say, however, we did not stay in the blind until dusk. We crawled out and waited in an opening until the land rover arrived to take us back to camp. Shannon didn't join me in any more blinds for the rest of the trip either. It turns out that the snake was a rock python—not venomous—but I'm not sure that if we had properly identified it earlier it would have made her feel any different. Crawling into dark ground blinds with only one exit were not in her planned future.

During that first safari, there was a great deal of discussion about snakes. Our host, Stewart Dorrington, would chuckle as he would relate a tale about this snake or that. He shared stories about a cobra in a bathroom occupied by his mother-in-law, and of a large python that crawled over him one night while he was in bed. Somehow it at got into the house, found a warm place, and decided to take up residence in the coiled bedsprings beneath Stewart. He said he couldn't really get back to sleep after the snake had crawled over him so got up and dispatched it with a .410. The over twenty-foot skin adorned a wall in the lodge. He also had a rubber mamba in a tree over the campfire pit and would share stories about them—the black mamba being one of the most dangerous snakes on the continent. He said that a test question to become a PH (professional hunter) quizzed about what treatment to use if a client was ever bitten by a mamba. The answer was a mixture of things, to include massive doses of antivenom, but in truth, he said the real answer was to drag the stricken client under the shade of a tree, so they didn't die in the sun. It was these stories that set the foundation for my initial wanderings around in the African bush. After about a week, I got a more personal lesson. I had hit a warthog well, and the blood was easy to follow. I radioed the lodge so a tracker would come assist in the recovery, but confident in the blood trail, I struck off before they arrived. I was being slow and deliberate in the trailing, and the PH and tracker arrived before I reached the boar and whistled me back to near where I had started. The tracker motioned me over to him and pointed down with a large staff at a blood-splattered dry leaf. Without saying anything (as I don't think he spoke any English), he flipped over the large leaf exposing a flat, hand-sized head of a large coiled puff adder. In my haste to follow up the spoor, I had nearly stepped on the creature. I lost a bit of nerve and opted to follow the tracker the rest of the way. We didn't encounter any more snakes, and it was a wonder to watch the skills of the man—not moving forward until he had taken in all that could be observed from what was immediately visible as well as in the distance. We found the warthog done in but not before it had backed into a large aardvark den (a long dark subterranean hole that I surmised could also be shared by other creatures).

My next trip to Africa was a couple years later, this time to a remote area in Mozambique. My good friend Rickey Davidson accompanied me on this trip, and we had left our homes near Kenai, Alaska in October 2002 to drive to Anchorage, fly to Minneapolis, then to Amsterdam, on to Johannesburg, and then to Pretoria, followed by a short night and then a two- and half-hour charter flight to a grass airstrip in a swampy savannah. Upon landing, we were greeted by the professional hunters and staff and were asked if we wanted to hunt some that afternoon. Only about three hours of daylight remained, and we were exhausted, having traveled for several days with little to no sleep. But we came to hunt, so hurriedly put our gear together and headed out into the bush before even visiting camp. Rickey and I separated with different professional hunters, and mine, along with a tracker, struck out along a well-forested area that bordered a vast open swamp. Soon we spotted twenty-six waterbuck bulls, and several of them were very large. At first, it didn't appear that any of them would present a reasonable stalk or shot opportunity given the openness of the terrain, but after a while, six of them, including the second largest bull, veered off from the herd and started feeding toward a small island of cover. We discussed the situation and decided to crawl out slowly into the vegetated island and try an ambush from there. We had a quick conversation too about the effective range of my fifty-eight-pound recurve, and of my desire for the PH to finish anything quickly with his rifle should I make a poor hit—not only during this stalk, but for any that might occur during the safari. I didn't care about record books, or number of trophies taken with a bow—only in ethical hunting and minimizing suffering. He nodded in agreement, and we began crawling carefully out into the swamp. Everything came together better than planned, to a point. We reached the cover without being detected, and the bulls kept feeding closer to our location. At slightly under forty yards, the largest bull stepped forward away from the other animals and turned broadside. It was near my maximum range, but I had practiced similar shots repeatedly and had complete confidence I could make the shot. I slowly got into a kneeling position and drew back to full draw—letting down a bit once, and then returning to my anchor point before releasing. The arrow looked good—headed straight for the pocket behind the foreleg, but then to my surprise, it struck the animal square in the ham. There was a slight breeze. Had the wind taken the arrow that far off mark? There would be plenty of time later to revisit what happened, but at that moment my PH glanced at me in a questioning way, and I nodded—meaning "shoot it." He raised his rifle and fired at the fleeing waterbuck, missing it twice before it escaped into the bush on the far side of the swamp. He took off rapidly, trying to catch up and get another shot, while the tracker and I went out into the opening and started looking for blood to follow. We had been at it for about fifteen minutes, slogging through alternating water up to our calves and relatively dry grass. I was scanning a few feet ahead, looking for blood, when I saw movement. A large Egyptian cobra raised up, fanned its head and neck out, and stared me in the face. The tracker saw the snake and yelled in broken English, "Cobra!" and turned and ran. I glanced down at the serpent, and then my bow, and quickly decided not to try and introduce the two. I remained frozen in place. The cobra did too, and then reduced his height a bit, relaxed his hood, then slumped back into the marshy grass and slithered away.

As darkness approached, I was reunited with the crew and taken to camp. Rickey and I were given separate thatched huts to sleep in. We were told that camp staff would sweep the dirt around them each day to help make sure that any snake belly tracks that approached the huts were both coming and going. This was some reassurance, that no unwelcome guest would likely appear from some hiding place while we slept, but it wasn't enough. Even though I was totally exhausted, I slept little the first night. When I turned out the lamp to try and sleep, the treetops outside came alive with the cries of bushbabies, and there was a great deal of scurrying around inside too. I would later discover that the hut was home to a goodly population of small rats (which undoubtedly were fine snake food). And then there were the bugs—moths mostly, but they were the size of small bats. They would flutter around and bump into my face or crawl around on the sheet I was covered with. Though I closed my eyes and tried to sleep, every time something brushed against me, all I could envision was that darn cobra. The next day was a long one (I'll finish the waterbuck story in the next chapter), but I prepared for sleep after nightfall with considerable forethought. I set rat traps (and caught several, including two in the same trap), wore ear plugs, draped a mosquito net over my bunk, and took two Benadryl. I slept like a baby for over ten hours.

BLACKBEARD

Blackbeard Island is barrier island off the coast of Georgia. It is a beautiful place of swamps and thick palmetto and surrounded by pristine white sandy beaches. It is rich in history, from rumors of Blackbeard the pirate hiding treasure there, to becoming a unit of the National Wildlife Refuge System, including a portion designated as Congressionally protected wilderness. It is also home to one of the oldest bowhunting venues in the United States, allowing only archery hunting to manage its whitetail deer population since 1947. Bowhunters have to arrive by boat during one of the three-day annual seasons (occurring in October and December) and then follow a set of rules that help make the hunt more successful. This primarily means no vehicle use on the roads—you need to walk from the campground to your chosen hunting blind—and hunters must stay at their blind from a half hour before sunrise to 9 a.m., and again from two hours before sunset until sundown. This means much of the walking about is done in the dark and temperatures during both hunts can be quite warm, meaning snakes can be quite active too. And when I say snakes, I mean rattlesnakes and water moccasins that seem to grow to near the size of telephone poles (well, not quite really, but they do get very big).

Since the island is a Refuge, hunters can only shoot deer, and more recently feral hogs that somehow made it to the island. Snakes are not allowed to be taken. This didn't stop a hunter a few years ago who killed a large rattlesnake and then placed it in the restroom at the camp to see what kind of reaction it would get from late night visitors who may have had too much hydration before retiring. The reaction, however, came from a Refuge employee who demanded that the snake slayer come clean or else he was going to suspend the hunt. The situation got unnecessarily out of hand when no one immediately came forward.

On a hunt there with Jim Hall, an old friend and former manager at Blackbeard, we set up on the far side of the island and had a great opening morning with Jim getting both a hog and a deer. He did run into a large water moccasin draped high up in the palmetto while dragging the animals out to a dirt road, but was no worse for the wear. Refuge staff drive around in a Kawasaki mule mid-morning and again right after dark, retrieving all game, and taking it back to the campground to hang in a cooler. Jim was feeling pretty good at the end of the day, knowing his animals were in the cooler, and he was joyfully taking long strides back to camp in the dark. Suddenly his steps increased substantially. Another large water moccasin appeared under his feet in the two-track and tried to become one with him. A few high steps and choice words occurred and the snake sunk into the bushes, having succeeded in its mission to slow our return to camp. We did slow our pace considerably, joking that the snake's purpose may have been to help feed its very abundant mosquito friends. But we agreed too, that a slower return allowed us to appreciate the beautiful starry night a little longer, though we didn't really look up that much.

Along with the abundant snake population, Blackbeard is also home to what I sometimes refer to as "big lizards." Alligators are regularly seen, and although they are generally docile, it is difficult to describe the sensation one feels when heading out in the dark with fading batteries in your headlamp and start to step over a log in the trail only to have it move. One tale of a Blackbeard bowhunter told of him encountering an aggressive 'gator that put him up a tree where he stayed until the sun set. Not knowing whether the animal had left or not, and not wanting to find out in the dark, he strapped into the tree so he wouldn't fall out if he dosed off, and spent the night. He was discovered the next day still in the tree, but the alligator was gone.

Big Blackbeard "lizard" – note armadillo in its mouth.

TEXAS

Texas is a great place to hunt. It has a wide variety of native game animals such as deer and turkey, as well as many exotic animals from Africa, India, and elsewhere. It also has lots of snakes. A good friend of mine grew up in West Texas—Mike Smith—and along with his two brothers, he kept the family ranch after they had all moved away and their parents had passed on. It was this old family property that provided many a good memory to me when invited to visit and hunt, primarily for feral hogs and Rio Grande turkeys. The first time I visited, I became aware of two concerns. The first was that if you wanted to have a beer, you needed to plan in advance, as Jones County was "dry" at the time. The second issue was the abundance of eastern diamondback rattlesnakes. They were not only numerous but also large, and very active as spring days warmed. This really only was a concern because of the necessity to travel in the dark to reach suitable turkey hunting areas before the birds flew off the roost. Walking rapidly through tall grass on a pre-dawn warm Texas morning, aided only by a dim headlamp, created all kinds of unique opportunities for close encounters with moving creatures. Usually, movement seen ahead was from a fleeing hog or armadillo, but my first thought frequently was that it was a giant rattlesnake. I was cautious on my first trip. On my second, I brought along a new pair of calf-length snake boots. I wore them for several days, but they were horribly uncomfortable so I eventually abandoned them and returned to using camo sneakers, and reverted to more cautious walking. Caution wasn't enough one day however. I was sneaking up to a small pond surrounded by brush and adjacent a lush winter wheat field. It was an area that nearly always held hogs during the heat of the day. I had a Brackenbury recurve in my left hand, an arrow out of the quiver in my right, and a pair of tennis shoes on my feet. I crept up on a fractured and slightly uplifted concrete foundation—all that remained of an old homestead. The whole part of my immediate surroundings came alive with rattlesnakes. Apparently, the foundation covered a den, or hibernaculum, and the concrete was retaining enough heat that the creatures desired to lounge on it, and around it, and under it. With buzzing everywhere, I looked for an escape, but snakes were already crawling out from behind me, so rather than back up, I just froze. About then, the granddaddy of them all appeared from under the foundation, and with only a slight rattle (compared to the frenzy of many others) proceeded to slither up from beneath the slab of cement and over my right foot, continuing past and disappearing into a patch of tall dry grass. After a couple minutes, enough of the others had followed that I was able to retreat the way I had come, and I abandoned the idea of hog hunting the area for the rest of the afternoon.

The next year I returned to hunt turkeys and hogs but had acquired new gear to guard against snakes. I had a new pair of camo-lined Kevlar chaps. They were a little stiff to walk in but otherwise worked pretty well. As the weather continued to warm the week I was there, I stopped wearing pants under the chaps. Instead, I would wear "Rhinoskins"—skin-tight long underwear that were designed to keep ticks from crawling past the cuffs at your wrists and ankles. Ticks could be another concern in the tall grass in the warmth of spring. One morning, I had set out a lone hen decoy on the edge of a field and then set back in the brush on a small stool and called occasionally with a stroke or two on a cedar box call. I heard a few gobbles in the distance now and again, but it seemed the boys were with hens and weren't likely going to approach any time soon. After a couple of hours of waiting, I felt the effect of too many early mornings starting to weigh heavy on my eyelids, and I slipped off the stool, laid my bow with a nocked arrow beside me, and curled up in a patch of tall grass. I fell asleep quickly and was out for twenty minutes or more when I woke feeling a strange sensation. Something heavy was working its way up my right leg—in between the ample gap between my Kevlar chaps and the skin-tight Rhinoskins. It slowed when it approached my knee, and then slowly pushed on. I leapt to my feet and danced a violent jig, kicking so high I would have made my Gaelic ancestors proud. The snake shot out into the grass—probably as upset as I was. As I gathered my thoughts, I glanced out into the field and saw a young Tom turkey also rapidly retreating past my decoy. I picked up my gear and called it a day.

RECIPES AFTER SUCCESS

While snakes may not be your first choice for a dinner entrée, they can be quite tasty. People may joke that they "taste like chicken," but I have found that they are more like fish, and can be used similarly. The one downside is the many bones, although large snakes have a good amount of boneless flesh along their back. I don't encourage or discourage anyone from shooting a snake—I have largely outgrown killing them, but they are an interesting prey that can provide unique skins for decorating bow limbs, as well as a good meal that is sure to keep dinner guests talking for quite some time. Of course, hunters need to be aware of local regulations. Some snake species are protected, and others have seasons and bag limits just like other game, depending on the state.

If a poisonous snake is to be handled, the head should be carefully removed and buried. I find too that skinning and gutting a snake is easier when they have been dead for a while—otherwise, they tend to squirm in a disconcerting manner, even with their head removed. This process can be sped up by putting the headless serpent in a cooler with ice or in the refrigerator (but make sure you have permission from your significant other before doing this). Once skinned and gutted, the snake can be cut into pieces about an inch long and then soaked in cool saltwater overnight. Dry with a paper towel, dip in lightly seasoned flour, and fry quickly in a skillet with hot oil. Keep the pieces spread out and turn once. Do not overcook—about three minutes should do if the oil is about 375 degrees when you start.

Author's son Remington with an unexpected addition to a January bowhunt.

CHAPTER FIVE

AFRICA

I suspect most hunters that really enjoy hunting, and adventurous travel, will at some point dream about traveling to Africa. Of course, Africa isn't just one place—it's a continent—a whole lot of different countries, game animals, habitats, and challenges. I have been fortunate to travel to Africa multiple times, and I would venture to say that many who plan their "once in a lifetime" trip to Africa find themselves planning another trip soon after their first visit ends, as I did.

African safaris are guaranteed to create lasting memories.
Photo by Shannon West

The first couple trips I took I used the assistance of Neil Summers of Bowhunting Safari Consultants. His insight and assistance were invaluable on my initial hunts to South Africa and Mozambique and the cost of his services were built into the fees I paid the safari operator. Speaking of cost (because that is often the first thing that comes to mind when contemplating an African safari), they are not cheap, but can still be affordable for many bowhunters with a little planning and budgeting. While it would probably be difficult to do so now, several of my African trips cost only a few thousand dollars total. I used airline miles for travel and was selective on what I hunted and what I did with the trophies I took. In general, the cost of an African safari is similar to or less than many North American hunts where travel and a guide's services are involved. One important consideration is that the listed trophy fees are only part of the cost once an animal is taken. Taxidermy, export permits, and shipping costs can be expected to double the price of what it takes to get a trophy from the veld to your wall.

Expect the unexpected in Africa.
Author's wife, Shannon, in the Karoo.

FIRST SAFARI

The year 2000 was special. While many worried about potential "Y2K" computer glitches that might occur as we faced a jump to a new millennium, others, including me, used the special time to justify a special trip. My wife and I, accompanied by life-long bowhunting companion David Mathiesen, scrimped, saved, and planned for over two years to take our first trip to Africa. We booked a ten-day safari to Melorani, a bowhunting only operation operated by Stewart and Bronwyn Dorrington. The day finally came that we landed in Johannesburg, cleared customs, and were met by Bronwyn outside baggage claim. She was initially concerned that our bows had been lost—she was used to seeing clients appear with large compound bow cases. We assured her that our takedown bows were in our luggage and all was well. We loaded up and began a several hour drive to the northwest, soon to have our first revelation that we were someplace totally different than we were accustomed to. After several days of traveling, including a long layover in Amsterdam, we were ready to relax in Bronwyn's care, and we let our heavy eyelids close easily as she drove. On the first occasion of awakening, and sleepily scanning the passing countryside, we were startled a bit to say the least. There were trucks and cars zooming right at us! It took a bit of getting used to everyone driving on the wrong side of the road.

After getting settled into our rondavels, Stewart gave us an evening tour of the area we would hunt, followed by a fabulous meal. We discussed our interests and limitations and plans were made for the next morning. In general, the days all started the same. We arose before dawn, helped ourselves to breakfast items laid out in the kitchen, packed a lunch, and were driven to a blind and left for the day. Stewart gave us each a radio. We were to call if we shot any game, if we wanted to move to another area, or if we wanted to return to camp. If we didn't radio in sooner, our pickup would be after dark. I didn't appreciate the freedom of this arrangement as much as I should have until going on other safaris in years to follow. In general, one can be expected to be accompanied by a professional hunter, trackers, or others (such as a government representative) when on safari. That can be okay too, but having the freedom to hunt as you want, where and when you want, and curl up and take a nap in the blind if you want, will always be my first choice. While Stewart advised that our best chance at success was to stay still in the blind all day, we were free to stalk outside the blind if desired. This I did every day. I shot nothing on such forays, but I enjoyed them immensely. Stewart did advise to use common sense when wandering. There were rhino and buffalo in the bush, as well as a variety of poisonous snakes, but all of that added to the adventure.

At first, the weather was moist and cool, and animals weren't moving much. Several days in various blinds did not yield any good opportunities, and the stalking, while exciting, didn't produce any shot opportunities either. On the fourth day, I sat alone in an elevated blind on the edge of dense cover. Most of the day had passed with little animal activity observed, but as the afternoon turned to evening, things changed. Animals were moving. A small group of zebras passed by, then a lone wildebeest bull, followed by some impala and warthogs. Then I saw two red hartebeest approaching. They were walking very slowly in my direction, and it seemed that they would come close to the blind. I hadn't thought about taking a hartebeest, but as I studied them, I made a decision to shoot if a good opportunity arose. It did. My arrow struck a young ram in the top of the heart, and it jumped high and sprinted away into cover. I pulled out the radio and called the camp. Soon, Stewart and a tracker arrived. The ram was found dead about forty yards from the blind and I had taken my first African animal with a bow.

First Africa harvest – a red hartebeest.

The first time in Africa is something difficult to describe. Everything is new—every sight, sound, and smell. If one is drawn to the natural world, you cannot help but stare in awe at the wonders and diversity of African flora and fauna. Having a bat-eared fox sit on its haunches and yip at you as the sun forms a giant orange ball before disappearing below the horizon, or a hornbill calling out from a mopane tree—disgusted at your presence, or a wildebeest snort from a patch of nearby thorn brush—that you had just snuck through (and were certain was devoid of any creature larger than an elephant shrew), all create lasting memories. Whether you release an arrow or not, I can't imagine anyone can honestly say that their first trip to Africa didn't exceed their expectations. We created countless memories, took hundreds of photographs, bought precious souvenirs, and were successful harvesting game too. David got a fine kudu, I got a kudu and a couple of warthogs, in addition to the hartebeest, and we all had the time of our life. There were plenty of close encounters too: the steenbok and wildebeest that wouldn't quite come into range, the sable and waterbuck that were in range but too pricey for my budget, and the ever-present impala that escaped both David and my arrows.

David Mathiesen and a fine bull kudu.

TECHNIQUES AND DECISIONS

Bowhunting for African species shares many similarities with bowhunting anywhere else. One has to figure out the best strategy for getting close to your prey and stay undetected while drawing your bow and releasing an arrow. There are some distinct differences too. In general, African animals seem tougher than North American big game, with some exceptions (for example I consider elk pretty tenacious to life and kudu rather "soft"). The point to this is that a poor shot may likely result in a lost animal in Arica. Most safari outfits employ some of the best trackers found anywhere on the planet, and some may use dogs too. These resources certainly aid in recovery, but a poorly hit animal may likely escape anyway. Another part of this equation is that most African antelope have their vital organs low and further forward than for North American game. A "right behind the shoulder" shot that would have put a deer or pronghorn down in seconds may be considered a "gut shot" on gemsbok or hartebeest and result in their loss. Patience and practice are critical. Arrows should generally be placed low and tight against a front leg of a broadside or angling away animal. In preparation for an African hunt, bowhunters should study online guides or get a booklet that depicts the anatomy of the animals they intend to hunt. One such guide is *The Perfect Shot* by Kevin Robertson (an African veterinarian). Make sure to study the graphics for all the animals, not just the ones you think you intend to hunt. Many a bowhunter has amended their trophy wish list while in the middle of an African hunt—sometimes in the middle of a stalk! Proper practice is also critical. If you will be hunting from a hide, practice often from as close to the same set up as possible. This could mean shooting from a sitting or kneeling position, as well as shooting through a narrow opening from a blind, and could be elevated or at ground level.

A final note about shot placement and recovery. Nearly every hunting situation you will encounter in Africa includes trophy fees to be paid when you shoot an animal. This doesn't mean recover an animal. If you draw blood, expect to pay. One can argue that some animals may recover from superficial wounds and a trophy fee should not be required. Don't try such an argument. Whether to charge or not is totally up to your professional hunter and they understand even a slightly weakened animal may easily fall prey to jackals or hyenas because of their wound. And no one wants to wound an animal, and we should do everything possible to avoid it. But if it happens, I suggest not letting it ruin your trip. I was given good advice once about such things suggesting that I plan on bringing the extra cash to cover for an animal that I might not recover—to part with the money without worry, and enjoy the rest of the trip to the degree possible.

Deciding what animals to hunt in Africa can be daunting—there are so many choices. Budget, of course may dictate much of your decision, but so will likely many factors such as the animal's appeal to you, and rules and regulations on take and importation (some animals have restrictions because of their rarity, like bontebok, and others because of potential disease transmission, such as birds, primates, and swine). Other factors may include the likelihood of success, either because of your abilities and/or the animal's abilities. For example, I have never worked up to a traditional bow weight that I would consider ethical to attempt to take a Cape buffalo. And I know that I could take many, many trips in pursuit of Vaal rhebok or klipspringer using fair chase methods and would likely never release an arrow. I do set goals for my hunts, but my primary goal is to always have fun while hunting ethically. I don't carry a tape measure or worry if an animal I might take would make the "book" minimum. I have great respect for people who have particular goals for a particular animal and of a certain size (and then prepare for and undertake their hunt accordingly), but that isn't me. I don't keep track of my score when I play golf either. I do understand that the greater challenge can equal a greater reward. Someone who makes multiple attempts only to finally be rewarded with success can be filled with elation. After bowhunting for over fifty years, I know what makes me feel good. Sometimes it comes from not taking an animal at all. In Chapter Four, I mentioned hitting a large trophy waterbuck poorly on trip to Mozambique. Days after wounding the bull, it was spotted with other bulls in a marsh about a mile and a half from where I had first encountered him. I was with my PH and Rickey Davidson and his PH. All of us were glassing the bull and it looked unimpaired—no limp—but it had a distinctive mark on a ham, a clear reminder of the three-blade broadhead I had struck him with. Other than a few flies buzzing around the wound, the animal otherwise seemed unaffected. Rickey had his rifle and he had wanted to take a waterbuck. This was a fine one and his PH recommended he take it. He declined—not being the way he wanted to hunt for one and we had several days left. His PH then turned to me and suggested I shoot the bull with Rickey's rifle. I would be paying the trophy fee regardless. I declined. That's not the way I wanted to take that waterbuck either. Whether the animal lived a normal life going forward or not, I was going to pay the trophy fee, but that didn't concern me at that moment. At a different time, I might have had a different response, but at that point I was fine with my decision, and I still am.

* * *

At some point in time, I decided I'd like to hunt springbok. They are a remarkable animal that are iconic to South Africa. They are prolific, small and swift, and traditionally are found in herds in wide open plains and areas devoid of much cover. My first attempt to take one was in the high veld of South Africa near the border with Botswana. I was taken to an imitation termite mound blind (made from brown fiberglass) and dropped off at first light. The structure was placed in nowhere particular—just in the middle of a vast open grassland. A few real termite mounds were in view, but nothing much else. As the land rover departed, I crawled into the blind, strung my bow, laid out my gear, and settled in. It took an hour or so of sitting and watching intently before the first animals came into view. There were black wildebeest and zebra in the far distance, a small group of gemsbok, and several groups of springbok. They all wandered aimlessly and fed where they wanted, stood and stared at nothing in particular, or occasionally bedded down. After a couple of hours of watching, I started to realize the likelihood of an animal passing close to my location was similar to finding a needle in a haystack. Still, every time a group of springbok started my way, I got hopeful. I had all day and the animals continued to move around and had to be somewhere—maybe some would eventually come close by pure chance? By early afternoon, I had stripped down to my underwear and felt somewhat foolish laying on the earthen floor of the blind almost nude. I had drunk most of the water I had brought and had only used my pee bottle once. My mind started to go from concentrating on looking for game out the small windows of the blind, to wondering how many bowhunters had been cooked in a brown cone-shaped fiberglass oven before. Fortunately, the heat of the day was short-lived and the sun dipped quickly later in the afternoon. I started putting clothes back on and paying more attention again, continuously peeking out the blind windows. Animals started stirring as well—getting up from their beds and feeding again. I noticed a herd of about thirty springbok slowly feeding my way. It seemed like an eternity for them to close any distance at all, but it was probably less than forty minutes before they were feeding about sixty yards from me. I watched them intently through my binoculars, while I knelt in the dirt and held an arrow nocked on the bow that was cradled in my lap. Fifty yards and closing. I started to get excited. Forty yards and feeding slowly closer. I squirmed around to get into shooting position. They wandered about—here and there— some a little closer, and some a little further—all too far, at bad angles, or with other animals behind. I glanced at my watch. I only had about an hour of shooting light left. As daylight faded so did the herd—ambling slowly away, undisturbed. At last light, a pair of jackals appeared, yipped noisily, and skittered past the blind, and then it was dark. Soon headlights appeared in the distance bouncing up and down as they got closer. I crawled out of the blind and shivered while I waited to be picked up. The temperature had dipped significantly, but I also was still shaking a little from the excitement of the day. Hunting springbok was clearly going to be a hurry up and wait type venture, but I was already thinking about my next chance to do so.

It was several years later that I got another chance to hunt them. This time I was in the Kalahari Desert and sitting in a box blind near a small waterhole. Unlike with a fake termite mound situated in some random spot, blinds near waterholes are more likely to create close encounters, if the wind cooperates, and you are patient enough. Most plains game desire to get water at least once a day. Because of this certainty, some question whether sitting over water is an ethical way to hunt. I understand this and my general preference, for all hunting, including in Africa, is to wander slowly through the bush while looking for game and then figure out how to get close once game is spotted. That said, I have taken game over water and can only say that each person must make a decision on what techniques are acceptable to them. My test is how I feel about taking an animal personally—both at the time of the shot and when animal is in hand. Taking a record class animal over bait would not be acceptable to me, whereas taking a small non-trophy animal after a long challenging stalk would be celebrated. Some would equate water with bait and in some cases I might agree. If there is only one waterhole and animals are limited to how they can approach (funneled right by a blind) that, to me, would be no different than shooting animals over corn (and of course many animals are taken this way too, legally in many places). Each person must decide what make them feel the best, and as long as it falls within legal bounds, I try not to judge others. For me, hunting over water is fine if it isn't the only water available and is large enough, without controlled access, so animals can come and go without necessarily being in range. Such was the set up in the Kalahari.

I hunted open grassland in the early morning, thick bush in the evening, and sat near the water in the heat of the day. Animals would come at irregular times. Some would linger near the water for long periods of time—others would sneak in quickly, take a quick drink, and disappear back into the adjacent thickets. Impala were the most common visitor, along with an occasional duiker. When a young springbok ram finally presented a shot opportunity, I didn't think about horn length. The Easton 2018 flew true from my forty-eight-pound Meigs longbow and fresh meat was soon to be roasted over an open fire in camp.

Springbok in the Kalahari.

TIPS

Safety is of course a major concern for most international travelers, so I want to discuss a few elements to consider while planning and undertaking an African safari. I have already discussed snakes, so won't talk about them too much more. They may top the list of some people's concerns in undertaking a trip to Africa, but while the continent is home to some serious serpents, chances are you won't see any, and if you do, it is unlikely they will give you any trouble. Many safaris are during our summer months, which is winter in Sub-Saharan Africa. There is less lush vegetation then, it is drier and cooler, and reptiles often are burrowed in somewhere and not very active. Pay attention to where you put your hands and feet and you should be fine.

There are some animals that deserve special mention when it comes to safety. Clearly when encountering any of the big five (rhinoceros, elephant, leopard, lion, and Cape buffalo), whether hunting them or not, special care is prudent. There is nothing that makes me more anxious, save maybe being charged by a grizzly bear, than being too close to an agitated elephant. Their sheer size and speed, accompanied by loud trumpeting and stomping of their enormous feet, should give anyone pause. Another of the big five that also sticks in my mind is an adult lion— you can watch one lying lazily in the grass, looking indifferently at you as you pass. The surroundings may be quiet and serene, but the animal understands it truly is the king of the beasts and you should too. When the animal decides to shift into its hunting mode, the world changes quickly—they are wickedly fast, determined, and deadly. Of the other big five, my encounters with buffalo have been numerous but rather brief. While they can present a problem at any time, the biggest risk certainly comes when hunting them (and making a poor shot). I think the same can reasonably be said about leopards and rhinos. Of course, you don't want to surprise any of these critters up close either. I once was strolling a two-track road before sunrise and stumbled over something in front of me. Upon closer examination, I realized it was rhino dung. I decided then to wait until daylight before moving any further—thinking it best to see what was ahead of me before getting too close.

Rhino dung is hard to miss.

Other African creatures that can do you quick and significant bodily harm include the crocodile and hippopotamus. Both can be quite common in some areas. No one should have to tell you not to go for an early morning dip in the muddy river near camp, or wade out to your waist in the same river, fishing rod in hand, in pursuit of tigerfish. Following such rules should prevent the vast majority of bad encounters with crocs, but hippos are another matter. They may generally spend their days lying in pools of water or sleeping at the water's edge, but they can also wander inland and bed away from water entirely. They also are reported to kill more people each year than any of the big five. Perhaps they feel threatened when away from deep water and act out in self-defense when surprised and not able to sink beneath the surface to escape perceived danger. Perhaps they can just be irritable and have bad days and decide to make toe jam occasionally out of a passing biped. I don't know. I do know they can weigh up to two tons, are remarkably fast runners, and the males have chisel-shaped tusks nearly as thick as my arm. Even knowing all this, I have to admit that I have never been overly frightened when seeing hippos up close, but then again, my encounters have always been with animals that laid quietly like giant stones sunning themselves, or simply disappeared beneath the surface of water when I got too close. Once, while hunting bushbuck in a mangrove swamp, my PH and trackers stayed behind so that I would have a better chance of stalking undetected. I slipped slowly along a dark and muddy streambank while scanning the area ahead only to hear a whooshing noise. I glanced at small pool of water a few yards away and witnessed a large hippo finish blowing air out its nostrils before slipping below the surface. I waited and watched it repeat a few minutes later—poking its head above the water ever so slightly, expelling, sucking in more air, and sinking back below the surface of the muddy water. When I returned to the waiting land rover about a half a mile away, I told the story. No bushbuck, I said, but I was rewarded with a unique encounter with a hippo. My PH broke out in Swahili addressing the chief tracker in heated discussion. Afterward, I asked him what that was all about. He shared that he was assured by the fellow that no hippos were in that area before agreeing to let me stalk solo into the thicket. I survived, no worse for the wear, and personally felt the risk was probably minor; however, I did take stock of the PH's concern, and logged it into my growing list of "watch out" items for when further exploring Africa on my own.

The most dangerous animal in Africa, in terms of harm to people, isn't lions or hippos or other large creatures. It is the mosquito. Somewhere between a half a million and a million people die of malaria each year in Africa. Add dengue fever, yellow fever, and several other viral diseases carried by mosquitos, and you should quickly decide to pack some DEET if you are headed into areas prone to disease-carrying insects. But as alarming as the statistics are, much safari travel occurs at times of year when it is cooler and, like with snakes, mosquitos can be dormant. Additionally, many Safari destinations have all but ridded themselves of malaria, including much of South Africa and Namibia. There are also some reasonable prophylaxes available, but they need to be in your system before exposure so be sure to talk to your physician about such things well before you travel. Your doctor should also be able to do a quick check on any inoculations that might be wise to get in advance of your trip.

Like with my initial naivety about snakes and hippos, I once thought of the malaria risk as minimal and that the agents coming onboard jets parked on airport tarmacs, and spraying insecticide in areas beside and over sitting passengers, to be overkill and perhaps unhealthy for more than just the potential insect hitchhikers. I remember experiencing this the first time on a British Airways plane in Johannesburg in route to London. I covered my glass of water and grimaced as they passed by. On a later trip, however, while refueling in Senegal, shortly after the agent passed by and "fogged" my row, I had a mosquito flutter down from who knows where onto the book I was reading and bounce around a bit on the pages. I instinctively crushed it only to leave a bright bloodstain on the paperback page—a lasting reminder that the threat of bloodborne diseases is real and reasonable precautions should be taken.

Other safety concerns include making good decisions about where and when you wander while in town, as well as while in the bush. Just like there being areas of Chicago you might be wise to avoid at 1:00 am, so too there are times and places you should avoid in various African cities, particularly the larger ones. Going to a store that is guarded by people carrying automatic rifles ought to give some warning that the area could be a bit dicey, but the best thing to do is ask your host before going out. Getting clients knocked in the head is bad for repeat business so expect them to be overly cautious, but that's okay. Pay attention to your gear as well as yourself. Don't wear expensive jewelry and flash around cash. Keep your passport secure and don't separate yourself from expensive optics or camera gear. You may be allowed two carry-on bags on your international flights only to find a connecting commuter plane to allow only one small item. Keep this in mind as you pack things like prescriptions and valuables. I have also had things removed from outside pockets that were unlocked on my luggage: simple things like a swimsuit, recently purchased souvenirs, and a small Swiss army knife.

A final word on safety is that you should expect and even welcome a little bit of uncertainty. It's all part of the adventure. Understand that flights are delayed and luggage is lost, safari vehicles get stuck and break down, and people get bitten by ticks and stung by bees. Plan the best you can, perhaps buy travel insurance that covers medical treatment and emergency evacuations, and then enjoy your trip and whatever it brings.

Lastly, I'll share some tips about tipping. You will almost certainly be well taken care of on your safari. Hours will be spent making meals. Laundry is often done daily. Skinners will work late into the night caring for trophies. Many people will be working behind the scenes to give you a quality experience. Sometimes too, professional hunters (your actual guide in the field) may be working primarily from what they earn on tips. Even though you may be spending several hundred dollars a day for the basic hunt, don't forget to tip. A candid discussion with the safari operator upfront on how many staff may be involved, and what normal tipping entails, is a good idea in helping plan your budget. Equipment and clothing can make nice gifts, but they don't pay the bills and shouldn't replace a monetary tip. That said, I once offered my PH a choice of cash or my takedown recurve and accessories. He gleefully accepted the bow. Part of the upfront discussion on tipping, beyond amounts, should include how the payments are best made. Foreign cash can be difficult to exchange in some countries or may even be illegal to have. Additionally, many operators prefer to divide up the tips among staff rather than having hunters sharing directly. This helps ensure fairness. Whether successful or not in taking the game you seek, much of the enjoyment of a safari is in the total experience: the people and the culture; the land and animals; and the food and transportation. The more you engross yourself in what Africa offers, the more you are likely going to enjoy it. You will make not only life-long memories, but life-long friends.

Enjoy all a safari offers.
Here, Rickey Davidson samples a coconut in Mozambique.

RECIPES AFTER SUCCESS

There is more good news than bad regarding eating African game animals. The bad news is you can't bring any meat home—not even biltong (jerky). Strict regulations govern the importation of meat, cheese, and other food items and they prevent sportsmen from bringing their edible prizes from overseas back to the United States. The good news is that you will most likely get multiple meals from the game you take while on safari, that those meals will be some of the best of your life, and that all the meat from animals you harvest will be used. Often, even the offal is utilized by local people, and I guarantee that game meat is never wasted. The only exception to using it for human consumption that I have ever seen was one safari operator selling some meat for animal feed—such as zebra to feed lions; however, I don't believe this is very common. Zebra is actually pretty good to eat, as is ostrich, warthog, and every type of antelope you might encounter. Even the very large animals are fully utilized. A Cape buffalo I took (with a rifle) provided wonderful meals of oxtail soup, roasted loin, and tongue sandwiches for people in our camp before being dried, stored in large flour sacks, and shared with local villagers, who were nothing but smiles when receiving it.

One recipe I'll share is a South African favorite: Monkey Gland Sauce. Don't let the name fool you. No monkeys or glands of any kind are involved in this sauce, and I don't know how it got its name. It is a sweet and tangy sauce that can be used to accompany any meat dish. The first time I tasted it was when it was drizzled over springbok backstrap cooked over an open fire in the Kalahari (see story above). Yum! Alter the following to match your taste (tabasco can be used to spice it up, etc.). Soften a finely diced onion in a skillet with 3 tablespoons of olive oil over medium heat. Stir in 2 teaspoons of minced garlic and then add ½ cup ketchup, ¾ cup red wine, ¾ cup spicy chutney, 1 tablespoon soy sauce, 2 tablespoons of Worcestershire sauce, 1 small can-diced tomatoes, 3 tablespoons of brown sugar, 1 teaspoon of ground ginger, and 2 pinches of salt. Simmer for at least twenty minutes, stirring often. Serve hot over steaks, roast, fish, or fowl.

CHAPTER SIX

LONE STAR OPPORTUNITIES

If there is one place in the United States that can mimic some of what can be found for hunting in Africa, it is Texas. It has huge savannah-like landscapes, sprawling scrubland, and rolling hills; it also has a vast variety of game, including many species native to Africa and other places from around the globe. Of course, it isn't quite the same—one has to choose carefully the type of hunt they are interested in and can afford—much of Texas hunting can be very expensive and the hunts can vary from chasing very wild animals over wide open and free ranging conditions, to "hunting" inside small high-fenced enclosures. While the latter may appeal to some folks, I have never done it, or hunted with anyone who has knowingly participated in any sort of canned hunt, so I honestly don't know much about it, accept it carries absolutely no appeal to me.

Texas has a rich history: claimed by France, Spain, Mexico, the Republic of Texas, then joining the United States in 1845 as the 28th state, and later being part of the Confederacy during the Civil War (collectively telling a story about the "Six Flags of Texas"). It is the only state, save those that comprised the original 13 colonies, that joined the Union without any federal public land. Texas was an independent republic, rather than a federal territory, and kept control of its lands. Large private holdings of land were developed for cattle as well as exotic game and Texans take their property rights seriously. For example, it is a felony to cross a fence without permission onto private land in Texas, if in possession of a weapon that could be used to take game. Poaching of a native deer and turkey would be bad, but shooting someone's breeding stock of sable or eland (worth tens of thousands of dollars) understandably creates some severe consequences.

*Texas has a large variety of native and exotic game,
including "wild" boar.*

I have been fortunate to have some Texan friends that have invited me to hunt their properties without charge. I also discovered a ranch a number of years ago that charged a very reasonable fee for access, and I found going there each November to be one of the more enjoyable things I did each year. An Engineering firm in

Houston had a hunting lease for forty years on a 10,000-acre cattle ranch in the Hill Country. For about $1,000, I would be picked up in Austin, driven to the ranch, given space in the bunkhouse, fed family-style meals, given transportation to hunting blinds, and enjoy some great comradery. The fee was for five days of hunting, but my host (Roger Krueger) always let me stay a week, since I was traveling from Alaska. The fee also included one whitetail buck and doe, two turkeys, and one hog. The property had a barbed-wire fence around most of it, but the game could come and go freely. A few free-ranging exotics were also found there on occasion, and a hunter could substitute a blackbuck antelope or audad ram for a buck deer if so desired. Part of the comradery was the willing hand of others to help with game once taken. These were not paid hands, just other hunters. A walk-in cooler, freezers, smokehouse, and grinding equipment was also made available. I always saved part of the last couple days of my hunts to process meat, and I always had help.

Decisions on hunting blinds were made first thing in the morning, well before light. Hunters would circle around a large black and white aerial photograph of the ranch that had sections and blind numbers drawn in. Each hunter would take a numbered token and place it over the area they wished to hunt. The chosen spot was then theirs for the day and they would not be disturbed by other hunters venturing into that area. I always waited until everyone else had chosen their blinds, and then I would take as much of a corner of the ranch that was left, and block it all off. While most of the hunters would go out just in the morning and again in the evening, and sit in a designated blind, I preferred to stay out all day and move around a great deal.

After a few years, I was given freer rein of the ranch and allowed to drive myself out to the hunting areas with one of the ranch vehicles. I remember well my first visit however, when I was an unknown and the entire ranch was unknown to me. I was picked up at the

Austin airport by Roger's son, Jay, and driven to the ranch after dark. I was briefly introduced around and then everyone went to bed. In the morning, staff and hunters alike were off doing their thing fairly quickly after a gigantic breakfast, and I was left alone to discuss my interests with Roger. I told him I was going to use a bow, and wanted to hunt for deer, but would take an audad if the opportunity presented itself. I was definitely interested in turkeys and hogs too, but they wouldn't be my focus. He smiled and said he thought he had a good place for me and we loaded up in an old Suburban and drove off into the darkness. He left me atop a brushy knoll where a stock tank had a small ladder placed over it to reach a half sheet of plywood that was nailed against an oak tree, about seven or eight feet off the ground. I was told that this was the only elevated stand on the property—everything else had been removed due to liability reasons. I was asked whether I wanted to be picked up for lunch and I declined, opting for an after dark retrieval. I was told to wander as much as I wanted but not to get lost because people wouldn't know where to find me. I grinned and waved as my host drove away. I strung my recurve and climbed onto the platform and waited for it to get light so I could see what the country looked like. At the first hint of light, there was a clamoring of hooves and a herd of audad appeared from the brush. There were seven or eight ewes and one mature ram. I didn't hesitate, drawing and releasing an arrow. It struck the ram a little above center not far behind the shoulder and penetrated about half the arrow's length. There was a blur of brown bodies rapidly departing the knoll and then all was silent. I waited an hour before climbing down from the stand, confident of my hit but wanting to help ensure the animal was down before starting to follow it up. At the time I had no idea how lucky I was to get the shot I did. I had been on the stand for only twenty or thirty minutes before the audad appeared. In the next seven years of hunting the ranch, and spending hundreds of hours, I would see few audad, and never come close to another shot.

I didn't know much about audad, also known as Barbary sheep, except that they were originally from North Africa and that free-range populations existed in parts of Texas and New Mexico. I also knew they had a reputation for being tough. I estimated the ram's weight at about 350 pounds. About the same as a bull caribou, I thought. I had ample time to rethink the shot as the hour past before I started tracking. Penetration wasn't what I would have preferred, but the shot was good. It would be fine. Normally the wait would seem long, but actually, the time went fast. The morning sun was revealing a new place to me. Scrub oak was thick, a prickly pear cactus was visible here and there, and there was a faint crimson glow to the light as it reflected off the orangish-brown-colored earth. A whitetail doe and young buck snuck by and a male cardinal landed on the ground below me. Soon it was time to start looking for the ram.

It is not uncommon not to find blood right away when first taking up the trail of a wounded animal. They can cover quite some distance on their first rush to escape, and certainly, the ram had done that. Usually though, within the first twenty or thirty yards on the escape path there will be a few sprinkles of blood, generally followed by a lot more in a few more yards, at least if the hit was through the lungs. I found no blood at twenty, thirty, and even forty and fifty yards out. At that point too, the ground was hard and there were no visible tracks, and game trails and passages through the brush were numerous. The sheep could have gone anywhere. At first, I moved slowly in the general direction that the animal had fled, looking ahead for any sign of the ram. I found none. After about an hour of zigzagging and searching every possible escape route and potential hiding spot within 200 yards, I returned to the blind. I sat for a while, had a snack, drank some water, and then took up the search again. I expanded my search area to a full 300 yards out and within

180 degrees of the initial direction the ram had taken. I kept at this for nearly two hours and found nothing—no blood, no hair, no dead ram. I was discouraged and returned to the blind. Was the animal fatally hit? Had the arrow only penetrated one lung? Did the ram lie down somewhere? Would I ever find it? I was discouraged but would not give up. It wasn't even noon yet; there was a lot of daylight left. I was getting ready to start my third search when I saw movement coming towards the blind. A lone whitetail doe cautiously stepped into the clearing, stopped, and then walked by nearly where the ram had been that I had shot earlier. I thought maybe I shouldn't shoot—I wanted the meat and the opportunity was good, but I had one animal hit already and I still needed to recover it. The doe stopped, my confidence boosted, and I drew and released. She ducked at the sound of the string as it propelled the arrow but was too late. It struck her through the spine and a lung, and she dropped in her tracks. No need to wait to follow up this one. I punched one of my deer tags, field-dressed the animal, and hung her in the shade. I then dove off into the brush again and started the search for the audad where I had left off earlier. This time I only went about fifteen yards and found the ram. He had died on a full run and piled up in a steep, rocky, area surrounded by thick brush. It was not a special place or a place of his choosing—just the spot where he ran out of air. Though the distance was a little over 300 yards, the animal still had almost certainly succumbed to the arrow in seconds. It just took me a while to find him. Unlike the doe, it also took me a while to field dress and cut up the ram. I could not drag it up the hill; I had to skin and quarter it and haul it up in pieces. This took some time, and when I finally got back to the blind with the first load, I was in for a surprise. The doe was gone. She had been hung on a sturdy limb with a good rope, but was no longer there. It wasn't Alaska, so I wasn't concerned with the thought of a grizzly. I looked in the dust nearby and saw boot tracks that weren't mine. No worries I thought. Someone from the ranch

had come and checked on me. I hung the audad meat I had been toting and headed back down the hill for more. The second trip was a little easier, but the last was a beast. I saved both the hams for the last haul, and I was tiring from a long day after a short night. It was now the heat of the day, and I stopped to rest a short distance from topping out by the blind. As I did, I heard a vehicle approaching. I finished the climb and met Joe Parsons, one of the nicest men you could ever meet. I had met Joe briefly the night before but knew him not at all. Yet he had taken it upon himself to come check on me, find the hanging deer and take it back to the cooler, and come back again. After brief story-telling, we loaded the ram and my gear in the truck and returned to the ranch. I had taken two animals with my bow on my first day in Texas and made a lifelong friend. It was a good day.

Audad ram.

* * *

In coming years, I would return to the ranch to hunt with old friends, and often made new ones. I took a nice whitetail buck with my bow and several hogs. I came close on turkeys but never connected. I do attribute later successes in hunting turkeys with traditional archery equipment to the many lessons learned there, but old Rio Grande gobblers eluded me at that location. The last time I went, I took my then eleven-year-old son Remington. He had not yet taken up hunting with a bow but was learning. He was able to harvest a nice hog with his namesake 7 mm-08 rifle and also made friends. A few of the hunters had been teasing him a little, and I remember the twinkle in his eye when we captured a turtle and slipped it into one of their sleeping bags in the bunkhouse. Rem waited impatiently for the surprise moment until we both got nervous and thought we should come clean. We let the unsuspecting fellow know that we had noticed his sleeping bag moving while we passed by (which technically was true), to which he responded, "That can't be good." We offered no more information but the turtle was soon discovered, released, and we felt a little better about not causing a heart attack or something that might be worse in retaliation, as there are many other critters found in Texas other than a turtle that one would not want to find in their sleeping bag.

RECIPES AFTER SUCCESS

This is the recipe I used to make chicken fried steak out of the better cuts of my audad ram. It was shared by the camp chef—a happy fellow from Louisiana who loved Cajun and Tex-Mex cooking almost as much as eating it. I regret I never got his recipe for smoked brisket.

Cut steaks as large as you want but only about ¾-inch thick and then pound them with a meat hammer until they are nicely perforated and no greater than ¼-inch thick. Dip them in a bowl of milk with a tablespoon of green Tabasco sauce mixed in. Remove drenched steaks, roll in flour seasoned with salt, pepper, and garlic powder and drop in a hot well-oiled skillet. Turn occasionally and cook until golden brown on both sides. Serve with fried potatoes, spicy red beans, and coleslaw (or anything you like)!

CHAPTER SEVEN

THE GRAND SLAM OF HAM

I don't know who first coined the term "grand slam of ham," but I have read stories from other bowhunters who have used it to reference the taking of four huntable species of pigs, or pig-like creatures: feral hog, javelina, warthog, and bush pig. Of course, the "grand slam" has long been used to describe the taking of each of the major varieties of North American wild sheep, but I assure you that the ham slam is easier on one's wallet, and more achievable for the average bowhunter (except maybe collecting a bush pig under fair chase conditions).

Pigs are found throughout the world—on every continent save Antarctica—and have long been a staple in the human diet and therefore a target of hunters before bows and arrows were even widely used. They are also ideal prey to pursue for modern bowhunters. Not only are they found widely, often there is little to no cost to hunt them, and seasons and bag limits rarely apply. They reproduce rapidly, are often viewed as pests, and can be very good to eat. They can also be relatively easy to hunt. They are smart but have poor eyesight; if one is careful with wind direction, it is often possible to approach very closely. This is especially true if they are fully engaged in feeding, or in the middle of a nap—both of which seem to be favorite pastimes. I never set out to complete "the grand slam of ham" or any other similar goal, but having now done so, I thought I'd share some of my thoughts about, and adventures with, swine and their kin from around the globe.

FERAL HOGS

All of the feral hogs available in the United States, whether labeled as such or given other names, like razorback, wild boar, European boar, or other, come from a common ancestry. Feral hogs are all given the scientific name of Sus scrofa and, most originally, came from Europe or parts of Asia, whether escaped from farms, transported by early Polynesians (to Hawaii), or introduced for hunting on private reserves. More states than not have feral hog populations, but the vast majority are found in states with warmer climates, especially Texas, Oklahoma, Louisiana, Georgia, and Florida. In most places, they are considered both invasive and destructive, and intensive management is encouraged.

Hunting feral hogs takes many forms, from hunting in a stand over bait to using dogs that find and hold them. While such methods can help increase harvest and meet management goals, there is also plenty of opportunity to employ still hunting or spot and stalk techniques to hunt hogs, and those are the methods I prefer. Not limited by a defined season, chasing hogs can be a great pastime all year to get outside, hone hunting skills, and add some meat to the freezer. Any hunting bow set up will work, as long as the shot is well placed and a razor sharp broadhead is used. Though not considered particularly dangerous, a cornered or wounded old boar has all the tools needed to do you harm. They are strong, fast, and equipped with extremely sharp canines. That said, the only close call I have ever had while hunting pigs was with a very large sow. I had killed a young boar and had field-dressed it when a sow, weighing perhaps 300 pounds or more, appeared nearby. I had no interest in taking another pig, let alone one I couldn't easily drag out of the field, so gave her only minor notice. But she clearly showed her intention as I was dragging the boar's carcass with one hand and holding my bow in the other. She didn't want me. She wanted the carcass but wasn't beyond giving me grief to get it. This may sound weird, and admittedly was an unusual experience (generally spooked hogs flee the area like a flushed covey of quail) but hogs are omnivores, and I suspect the sow didn't attain her size by eating only grass. I shouted and threw a few rocks in her direction before nocking an arrow and standing my ground. She backed off, just out of effective bow range, but did not leave. I resumed my dragging, and she followed at a distance until I came to a fence line and pulled the carcass under the barbed wire. Still, I looked over my shoulder frequently before reaching my vehicle. She was still out there somewhere, doing whatever a hungry "devil pig" does. I was reminded of the old unsavory response to a query of where someone was: "He went out to take a sh. . . and the pigs ate him." Honestly, the experience didn't slow my interest in hunting hogs, though I was more thoughtful of where I stretched out for short afternoon naps while in the field.

Feral hog.

JAVELINA

Second to feral hogs, javelina (also known as peccaries) are the most available component of the grand slam of ham. Though managed with seasons and bag limits, like all native game species, there are ample opportunities to pursue them in Arizona, New Mexico, and Texas. While they look like pigs, and share many of the characteristics of them, javelina are an ungulate, not a true pig. They primarily inhabit southwestern deserts and scrubland and have a relatively small home range, providing hunters some certainty that their intended prey is close by if abundant fresh sign is discovered. This includes tracks and scat and also includes shredded plants (usually the base of tubers or cacti or the pads of prickly pear). It also includes small holes dug in the desert floor left from searching for succulent roots and other food. Once abundant sign has been found, the best hunting technique is to find a good vantage point and glass far and wide early and late in the day. Proximity to water can also be a real plus. Javelina are often in small herds, but it is not uncommon to find boars alone or in small bachelor groups. While size, coloration and behavior can help distinguish a sow from a boar, the only sure way of knowing the gender of the animal is examining it after you have tagged it.

Spot and stalk techniques are usually the most productive, but I really like tracking javelina across the desert immediately following a good rain. Their tracks are small—a piglet track is not much bigger than a dime and even a big boar has a squarish track of less than two inches long, but they stand out well in soft sand, particularly when a herd is involved and the tracks are all in a line. In my early years hunting javelina, I largely kept my searches to cactus patches and dry washes; however, over the years, I have found them many other places too, from steep rocky slopes to open fields and forested areas. Like anything else, you only will find them where you look. Another technique for hunting javelina includes the use of a predator call. The crying rabbit sound also mimics the noise made by a distressed pig-let and can draw the attention of a protective herd. In full disclosure, however, this technique has helped me fill my tag on two occasions, but in many more instances, it resulted in the herd "beating feet" without looking back.

Javelina are a great animal to start fledging bowhunters on. Success rates are generally high, and as they are small, a heavy bow is not necessary. While not difficult to kill, the acceptable target is rather small. There is simply a lot of head, mid-section, and butt on javelina. A shot tight behind the shoulder is best, and if properly executed, the animal rarely goes far, and often expires quickly right where shot. Like feral hogs, adult javelina come equipped with a nasty set of teeth, and they will frequently posture and pop them when they feel threatened. They do this while making a woofing noise, raising the hair up on their back, and emitting a noticeable musky odor. This can be intimidating, but rarely results in harm to anything. This can be different if you have a bird dog that gets too close while chasing desert quail, or if an animal is wounded. I have had two javelina give me pause over the years, and both were because of poor shooting on my part. The first was a large boar that I had hit too far back. He retreated into a cave-like thicket of mesquite and catclaw and I followed slowly, pushing my sixty-inch recurve ahead as I crawled. I was able to make a follow-up shot by lying flat on my back and pulling to half draw. The technique didn't matter much as the boar was only a few feet away. It did quickly dawn on me, how-ever, after releasing the second arrow, that the only escape from the brushy cave was the way I had crawled in. The boar knew this too, and as the arrow struck him, he boiled over me, snapping very long and sharp tusks as he departed. I pushed him away with my bow as he ran by, and fortunately, he didn't delay his escape to teach me a lesson. I found him piled up about thirty yards away.

The other instance of a javelina that chose fight over flight was also the result of a less than ideal hit, but I didn't know it immediately. Hunting buddy David Mathiesen was above me several hundred yards making a stalk on a Coues whitetail buck when I noticed a group of sleepy javelina get up from tall grass and reposition themselves, plopping back down below me. Having both Arizona deer and javelina tags in my pack, I made a quick stalk and sent an arrow into one of the animals. It sprinted briefly away and went down in an opening at the base of a tree. I turned my attention back to David. He was still sneaking forward around the rocky knoll above, but I could see the buck's white tail flagging his departure hundreds of yards away when David couldn't. This was a familiar sight for us, and most of our attempts at stalking the desert gray ghosts ended similarly. I rechecked the downed javelina below and then climbed up to intercept David. We shared a few stories and then descended together to recover my javelina. As we approached, I looked again through my binoculars and should have been alerted. The animal was motionless but its eyes were closed. Most expired animals have their eyes open, or at least partially so. I did have an arrow ready on the string, but it didn't matter. As we closed the distance, the stricken peccary hopped up and took off. David and I gave each other a quick glance and then took off in pursuit. The country was open ahead, and it seemed there was little chance that the animal could escape. It must have sensed that too, for after a few moments it stopped and turned, and then came charging back right at us. While David and I had much to discuss later, no words were uttered then. We both drew and quickly released arrows, and amazingly, they both struck the animal in the skull and killed it instantly. I didn't know what to feel. On one hand, I was glad to have finished the job quickly and fill my tag. On the other hand, I couldn't help but feel a little remorse for killing an animal with such courage. But then again, it is possible it just was indecisive, not seeing any escape cover ahead, and wasn't charging at all. Only the javelina knew for sure, but David and I have retold the story enough that the world now knows that we are fantastic shots with our bows when under pressure (or maybe just lucky).

Javelina.

WARTHOG

Desiring to branch out from hunting only in North America, I traveled to Africa, and there had many great adventures. Not interested in taking dangerous game with a bow, I focused on abundant plains game and one of the most abundant, and fun to hunt species, is the warthog. They are not only plentiful in many areas, but are stalkable, good to eat, affordable, and make wonderful trophies. The ivory tusks of a mature warthog far exceed what are found on other swine and the skull or mount of an old boar are truly impressive.

Like most other swine species, warthogs are diurnal—they are most active in mornings and evenings. But it is not uncommon either to find warthogs active in the middle of the day, either feeding intently, or moving to a water hole for a drink. Because of this, hunting them can be accomplished well by either waiting in ambush or by spot and stalk. It is important to note that while warthogs appear big and clunky, they are extremely fast and are well-known for "jumping the string," which isn't really jumping at all, rather, at the sound of the release of the arrow they lunge forward and drop down. As such, it is not uncommon to aim and release perfectly only to have the arrow strike a little high and too far back. This you never want with any animal, but with warthogs, it is extremely challenging as they are tenacious to life and anything but a perfect double lung hit can result in a difficult recovery or lost animal. There are some mitigating factors one can employ. I would like to suggest just aiming low and in front of the shoulder, but each hog's reaction to the release of an arrow can be different, and besides, who can aim for a place they don't really want to hit? Instead, avoid extremely close shots (where the animal is likely to "explode" at the shot), shoot the fastest set up (in terms of bow draw and arrow weight) that you can effectively use, and use the best string silencing arrangement possible. Equally important is knowing when to release your arrow. Don't shoot at an animal that is fully alert. This can be an animal that has just heard, seen, or smelled something they don't like, or one that just arrived at a waterhole. They seem to know they are vulnerable when drinking, and predators like to lie in wait by water. Best yet, try to take shots at hogs that are feeding intently. Sometimes they will even kneel when feeding and this provides the very best shot opportunity because of their inability to move quickly out of that position.

To emphasize my point about how tough warthogs can be I won't share a story about any that were successfully taken, but rather, about one that got away. David Mathiesen and I were hunting in

South Africa on a ten-day safari and always hunted apart from each other, so we didn't know how the other's day went until we were back at camp after dark. One evening, David came in a little late and shared that he had arrowed a monster warthog right before dark. The PH and he agreed to wait until daylight to look for it because the area was very thickly vegetated. It was also full of aardvark dens and the hogs frequented them, whether wounded or not. Dealing with the recovery would be much more manageable in the light of day. David relayed the shot in detail. The boar was close to his stand and the shot looked good. He had placed a heavy 2219 aluminum arrow from his seventy-two-pound longbow right behind the shoulder and saw it protruding out the far side as the animal departed. He also said that blood, lots of blood was immediately evident after the shot—easy to see, even in the fading light. David is calm and competent and given to detail. We were certain that we would find his animal as soon as it got light.

We were at the stand at first light where David had shot the evening before. The trail was easy to follow. Bright red blood was sprayed abundantly on both sides of the tracks. Soon we found the arrow—corkscrewed and covered with blood. We went further and the blood became less but still obvious. A little way beyond, there was a substantial pool of blood where apparently the boar had stood watching its back trail for some time. Beyond that point there was no blood. We stood still there for a while and listened. At one point, the PH motioned to a thicket where a faint blowing noise could be heard. He said softly, "That's him—breathing with only one lung." Sneaking around to look we quickly discovered his error. The noise was coming from an agitated puff adder. David commented, "That really chills my sh. . ." We retreated slightly, and the PH went to the truck and came back with Binga, a female Rhodesian ridgeback that was well versed in tracking. She disappeared on the track into the bush, and it was not long before she found the wounded boar. We could not see into the thicket but we heard the commotion. Binga yipped loudly and came running back to us. She had been cut by the boar's tusks. The wounds were very noticeable but fortunately not very serious. The PH took the dog back to the vehicle and then returned to work ahead of us with his rifle. David and I carried our bows and tried to study the ground for sign while keeping the PH in sight. My wife Shannon tagged along too. She wasn't armed but wanted to be in on the effort. At some point she wandered through some thick elephant grass and got covered with ticks—hundreds of them. The PH took the wounded dog and my ticky wife back to camp, and David and I continued to search. We never found the wounded warthog, and though discouraged, wondered if it wasn't a good thing. The area was so thick that any follow-up shot would have been very close, and the boar was likely still very active, and likely very ticked off.

When an animal is shot and not recovered, there can be a lot of emotion. Sometimes, rationalization comes to play. You might say that you think the animal will likely recover and be fine. In some cases, that is probably true, but others, it is not. We rarely ever know. The only thing we can do is our best to make an ethical shot in the first place and then our best to recover it once hit—no more—no less. Both of these standards were met with Davd's warthog. Perhaps it backed into an aardvark den and slowly slipped away—to become food for jackals and caracals? Or perhaps it lived on to challenge another bowhunter or whip another dog?

Warthog.

BUSH PIG

The last entry into the ham slam diary is the bush pig. These hairy and medium-sized swine species are found through much of sub-Saharan Africa and share many of the same traits as their cousins. They are less common than warthogs and tend to be more nocturnal. This makes getting one more difficult, and many hunters may resort to hunting over bait at night, or use dogs, to aid in their success. I was lucky to take my one and only bush pig under fair chase conditions. This wasn't so much the effort I put in as much as being in the right place at the right time.

It was about 4:30 a.m. when my PH and trackers followed me down a grassy path that led to the river. It was light enough to see where to put my feet, but not light enough to see any features of the jungle or animals that were more than a few yards away. The Mozambique morning was dimly lit anyway. The rising sun penetrated a light smoke that lay close to the ground. Distant villagers were burning extensively. Some of the reason was to promote agricultural activities, but mostly, it was a traditional effort to set back the ever-growing jungle and create clear passage for people desiring the ease of travel as well as provide adequate visibility ahead to spot potentially unfriendly wildlife before getting too close. Treetops came alive as birds took wing at my approach, but I saw little else for the better part of an hour. The PH, armed with an iron-sighted .450 Watts, trailed me about 100 yards back, along with three trackers. We had previously agreed that I was unlikely to be successful stalking game with an army alongside, but that I would always try and keep them in sight (though that really was more their job). I stopped as I saw movement in the palmetto ahead. A large orangish bush pig appeared momentarily and then disappeared just as quickly. I removed an arrow from my bow quiver and crept slowly forward. I was already within my comfortable shooting range and knew this was an animal I wanted to take. All I needed was for it to provide a clear shot. When it did, I had an arrow on the way quickly, and it found its mark. I released two more as the boar grunted and spun in a circle. The animal succumbed in seconds and fell where he had stood when I first shot. The PH ran up to me and the pig. He was out of breath but wore a huge grin. Soon, the trackers joined us and were also quite cheerful—more so it seemed than with other animals I had taken. I asked why. The PH explained that bush pig was the best eating animal in the jungle, and everyone was going to be very happy in camp. Whether it was the best meat around I do not know, but it was very good, and my mouth still waters a little when I think about one particularly nice roast, glistening with fat and well-seasoned with salt and black pepper.

Bush pig.

RECIPES AFTER SUCCESS

Pig meat can be delicious. I do recommend avoiding big boars when shooting feral hogs if you are primarily interested in the animal's culinary value. As they get older, the males tend to get tough and sinewy and take on an odor. They can still be used for chili and taco meat, but you probably would be happier overall with a young boar or sow if your primary goal is putting meat in the freezer. I have not found the same caution to be true with javelina, warthog, or bush pig. There are countless good recipes for cooking pork, making pork sausage, or smoking bacon or hams. Not all wild swine can be used equally for these dishes, but most can. The key factors are having clean, odor-free meat, and at least some natural fat (also clean and odor-free). Another factor in preparing all swine is to cook it thoroughly to avoid potential disease. One of the easiest dishes to make, and one of my favorites, is pulled pork.

Clean and cut about two or three pounds of pork into chunks no bigger than an egg and place in a crockpot with enough water to cover the meat. Season with salt, pepper, and garlic powder and add one large diced onion. Let the crock pot heat to a slow boil and then cook on medium for two hours. Drain the water and start again with a fresh diced onion, two teaspoons of liquid smoke, and two cups of red wine—adding water as needed to cover the meat with an inch or two of liquid on top. Mix well and cook on low heat for six to eight hours, until tender. Drain liquid, saving about one cup, and place meat in a large bowl and shred by pulling the pork apart using two forks. Add the meat, saved liquid, and one bottle of your favorite barbecue sauce back into the crockpot and cook on high for one hour. Serve on buns and have napkins ready!

CHAPTER EIGHT

MORE OFTEN THAN NOT

One of the realities of opting to hunt with traditional archery equipment is that it may take many more days to fill your tag than if you use a rifle or even a compound bow. You should except often as well, that the trophy of a lifetime may escape unscathed, and frequently, you may not fill your tag at all. If these things are bothersome to you, using a stick bow as a primary weapon to hunt may not be the best choice. Sometimes, the failure to bring home game is totally a personal choice—you choose not to take a shot that you have confidence in. Other times, even though you hunt hard, opportunities just don't present themselves. And then there is the third category. This includes the situations in which you get within range of your prey, have every intention of taking the animal, but something goes wrong. These are often long and drawn-out encounters at close range, and they can provide deep and lasting memories—memories that are fun to relive and share, but which can also form seeds of desire to try again—to accept the challenge and plan to do differently and better the next time.

I suspect I am not alone in experiencing hunts, that are repeated, perhaps often, but just don't ever seem to produce the hoped-for results. If taking game was the only thing that motivated bowhunters to go afield, this could be an issue, but it rarely is. Creating memories with friends or family in wild and wonderful places, having even the slight possibility of harvesting an animal, is more than enough for most of us to go again and again, whether we ever fill a tag or not. I have certain species that have continued to illude me with my recurve or longbow, namely, Dall sheep and Coues deer. I also have some locations, with multiple species pursued, that have produced the same result (nada), and my absolute favorite unsuccessful hunting locale is New Zealand. I have taken multiple trips there, have spent nearly two months of climbing the Southern Alps or crawling through wet ferns and vines in rainforest, and have little to show for it, but I'd go again in a heartbeat.

KIWI COUNTRY

My first trip to New Zealand included two hunts on the South Island. I was picked up at the airport in Christchurch by Kiwi friends Philip and Janet Commins, as well as Jim and Holly Akenson, who had arrived shortly before me. We drove to a remote sheep station situated in a broad river valley and set up a tent camp. The backdrop to the camp was a steep mountain range that held Himalayan tahr—our intended prey. While rare in their native habitat, tahr have thrived in New Zealand. They, like all of the introduced big game animals in the country, require no license or tag to hunt and have no season or bag limit.

On the first morning we were to hunt, I woke before dawn and started assembling gear by the light of my headlamp in my cramped two-person backpacking tent. It was still cool, as well as dark outside, and no one else was stirring yet, so I stayed in my down sleeping bag while putting together my takedown bow. Once assembled, I picked five arrows from their case and carefully affixed razor-sharp Phantom broadheads. I say careful, as I was slow and deliberate to avoid cutting myself as I removed them from their padded box and tightened them onto the tips of the arrows. At some point, however,

I wasn't careful of my surroundings as I punctured the tent ceiling and fly while maneuvering an arrow into my bow quiver while lying prone. I was upset with myself at first and then chuckled, thinking, "That's what duct tape is made for." I got dressed and crawled out of the tent with my bow loaded and ready for tahr.

Holly and Janet remained tucked into their sleeping bags while Philip, Jim, and I ate a hurried breakfast and started out in the dark across the floodplain to the base of the mountains in the distance. Once there, we started to climb. The slope was steep and seemingly never ending. I was no stranger to climbing mountains, having chased Dall sheep and mountain goats in Alaska for years, but this was different. Perhaps I was dehydrated after days of traveling? Jim, also well versed in maneuvering mountainous terrain, struggled too, but Philip seemed to be part tahr himself, scrambling with ease upslope and stopping occasionally to grin and beckon us on. Nearly to the top, Philip spotted a small group of bulls. Jim hung back and worked slowly around the slope, while Philip and I preceded slowly upward. When we were less than 300 yards from the herd, Philip advised for me to work around a cliff edge, out of sight of the animals, and try to get in front of them. After a while, he would continue upwards and hopefully push them to me. The plan worked perfectly. I waited, arrow nocked, while crouching at the edge of a small thicket overlooking where I thought the tahr might appear. I heard rocks rolling then saw one bull, and then another, and then two more. They all moved into view directly below me and were looking back toward Philip. They were less than thirty yards away, broadside, and unaware of my presence. I picked a spot behind the shoulder of the closest bull and drew and released. The angle down to the target was extreme but the arrow flew true and struck high behind the shoulder. I heard the shaft clamor off rocks below as the it passed through the animal and I felt a sense of accomplishment. I climbed down to where the animals had stood as Philip appeared below. I saw the herd in the far distance running full out over the top of the mountain and I pulled up my binoculars to take a final look. All of the bulls were there, and all running without difficulty. Hmm? I started looking for my arrow. What I found was a patch of golden-brown hair nearly twelve-inches long. Though I had clearly seen the arrow disappear high into the animal's chest, these were the first tahr I had ever seen, and I didn't know that they had such long manes of hair over their neck and shoulders. What I thought was a high lung hit had done nothing but shave hair. To this day, when I lay in my old two-person backpacking tent and gaze up at the duct tape patch, I see the long mane of a tahr moving magnificently in a Southern Alp's morning breeze, and I smile.

* * *

After we left tahr country, we drove south and chartered a helicopter to take us into the fjordlands in pursuit of red deer. We expected the stags to be roaring, and we were not disappointed. We camped beside a large river and hunted mostly upstream as the river was too large to cross, and the adjacent areas were very steep or were covered with nearly impenetrable vines, ferns, and thornbushes. I was new to red stag hunting, but was intrigued with the creature. The similarities to chasing elk were obvious and also very different. I made myself hoarse trying to imitate the guttural throaty scream of a roaring stag, whereas I had given up years ago bugling for bull elk, instead only producing an occasional soft cow call when approaching a herd. I had learned that my elk bugling expertise was far more likely to send a bull running away than enticing him to me. I had similar results with my roaring for stags, but I had fun trying.

Given enough time wandering the rain forest, close encounters with stags came, even though my prowess with calling was lacking. There is nothing quite like having an adult red stag ten yards away, standing regally and roaring repeatedly, and be unable to draw your bow, so you just stay motionless and take it all in. Some of the encounters were a surprise to me—all of a sudden, the deer would appear and I could do nothing but freeze in place, watch, and wait. And some of the encounters were result of carefully executed stalks, that were successful in getting close, but produced no shot, generally because of extremely thick vegetation. In one case, I was no more than eight yards from a stag for a few moments before it moved away and out of my view. With my heart pounding, and arrow nocked, I saw only part of the stag's legs, the top of its antlers, and a bit of reddish-brown blur in between.

The time in the fjordlands went by quickly. Jim had an "almost" with a stag, and Philip passed on some smaller animals, but no venison was hanging by the time the helicopter returned to pick us up. It was with mixed emotions we prepared to leave. The near constant rain had left nearly all of our gear damp, and when things warmed, even a little, the sandflies took it as a sign that it was time to feed. But as the craft lifted off, and we peered back down upon the forest below, we knew that the stags were still roaring, and we longed to be back in the midst of them.

* * *

My last hunt in New Zealand started with a trip to Stewart Island, a 674-square mile wild area located about nineteen miles south of the South Island. Actually, it started with a flight to Portland, Oregon where I connected with Jim and Holly and Hanley Jenkins. From there, we caught a flight to San Francisco, then Auckland, Christchurch, and Invercargill. In Invercargill, we were met by Janet and Philip and shuttled to Bluff where we would board a charter boat to take us to Oban to spend the night. The same charter then would take us to a remote bay with a cabin and, weather permitting, pick us up ten days later. The travel was not without certain difficulties. We had trouble transferring our bags in San Francisco, literally walked onto the plane to Christchurch as the door was closing, and discovered at baggage claim in Invercargill that one of our bags missed a connection somewhere. The bag happened to be Holly's and included her sleeping bag. Arrangements were made to have the bag sent to Oban and dropped off days later by the charter boat at our cabin. We pooled our gear to help Holly be as comfortable as possible in the meantime. The most memorable part of the travel to Stewart Island however was the wind. Seeing an overturned truck along the road from Invercargill to Bluff was our first indication that it was more than just a little breezy, along with having to hold onto our hats as we exited the airport. I was pretty sure the boat would not be sailing, but I was wrong. The boat was seaworthy enough, but rocked violently as we plowed through the choppy seas toward Oban—waves lashed at the sides of the vessel and spray leapt upward and over the boat. It was a real "puker"—many of the passengers lost what food their stomachs carried and I wish I had. It might have given some relief. As it was, I wobbled off the boat when it finally docked, pale and green and unsure whether I was going to eventually throw up or just curl up and die first. I survived the night and fortunately the weather settled down by the next morning so that the short boat ride around the island was actually enjoyable.

Stewart Island does not have populations of exotic game animals that one would normally travel around the world to pursue. In fact, our intended prey on the hunt was whitetail deer—exotic for New Zealanders, but certainly not for seasoned hunters from the United States. It was not the deer that drew us to the island however—it was its remoteness, beauty, and unique creatures. It is one of the few places in the world where one actually has a reasonable chance of seeing a brown kiwi in the wild—in the forest, or even probing the beach sand with its long bill. I mention this because my most memorable experience of the trip was while I was sitting along a deer trail in dense forest and hearing an animal approach. I nocked an arrow and waited motionless only to see an adult male kiwi wander into view. When only a few feet from me, the bird tilted his head skyward and let out a loud and long high-pitched repetitive trill for nearly thirty seconds. It was simply amazing.

Brown kiwi on Stewart Island.

Philip, Jim, Hanley, and I were all hunting, while Janet and Holly spent their days hiking and exploring. Given the amount of time we were to be on the island, and that all four hunters were experienced, we had planned on supplementing many a meal with fresh venison. It is a good thing that fish were abundant in the bay, and abalone available from the rocks at low tide. We had wonderful meals with plenty of protein, but not a lick of deer meat. The stories, and there were quite a few, always went something like this: "There I was, crouched and ready as the deer finally turned and provided the perfect shot. The arrow was on its way—straight to the vitals—but then it bounded away, unscathed. . ." A lengthier account would describe how the deer "jumped the string"—the same misnomer I explained relating to hunting warthogs. The animals react to the noise of the arrow being released, not by jumping in the air, but by flattening out. At such close ranges, and given the incredible reflexes the deer had, a perfectly aimed shot routinely flew over the back of the animal, or at best merely shaved a little hair. After a repeat of this scenario, you might think one would change tactics. Perhaps by just aiming a little lower? Of course, that is difficult to do, and in any case, we repeated what came naturally, and the results were predictably the same as well. I imagine the deer of Stewart Island may still be snickering about the old guys with the sticks that invaded their turf for ten days.

Stewart Island gang – left to right: author, Jim and Holly Akenson, Philip and Janet Commins, and Hanley Jenkins.

Following the trip to Stewart Island, we made two red deer hunts on the South Island and a fallow deer hunt to the north. Each adventure produced close encounters, but I did not release an arrow.

If Philip hadn't shot a fallow hind for meat on our last full day of hunting, a month would have passed without any bowhunting success. But that isn't how we measured success. We shared countless adventures among good friends, in unique and beautiful places, and created wonderful memories to last a lifetime. What could be more successful?

THE BIRDS AND THE BEAR

In later years, I always bought the Sportsman's Pac when acquiring my annual licenses in Oregon. This provided a plethora of authorizations to pursue everything from mountain lion to shellfish. It was with this knowledge on an Oregon elk hunt that I knew I had an unfilled bear tag in my pack, keeping my archery deer and elk tags company, when a large black bear suddenly appeared in front of me. Not that I was looking for a bear. In fact, when I first spied the animal, I had no interest in anything but watching it.

It was late into the second week of the season. Elk encounters had been frequent, but no meat was hanging in camp. I had struck off before daylight with Rickey Davidson in hopes of chasing bugles, but the morning was quiet. We did find however, where a large herd bull had pushed some cows through a swampy creek bottom sometime during the night. He had torn up small trees along the way, and there was even a bit of musky smell in the wind lingering from his passing. The herd's tracks were easy to follow so we set off slowly in pursuit, scanning the timber ahead for the tell-tale sign of dark legs, yellowish brown bodies, and creamy butt patches. We never caught up to the herd—not an uncommon outcome when sneaking behind a group of elk that are moving from their feeding to bedding areas. We removed our outer layer of clothing as the day warmed and decided to split up and work our way separately back to camp. It was mid-morning then, and Rickey and I hadn't parted for more than fifteen minutes when I saw a bear loping my way from Rickey's direction. It slowed when it reached the patch of cover that I was working and stopped to stare back in the direction from whence it had come. The bear was large and dark and blended in well with the tangled timber in the creek bottom. I watched it through my small binoculars for a minute or so and processed the notion of trying to get some bear meat. This was not an easy decision. I much preferred elk over bear meat, the weather was warm, and if I shot the bear, I would have to take a couple days off from pursuing elk to take care of the meat. Still, a "bird in the hand" I thought, and I nocked an arrow. I raised the binoculars again and studied the animal which had stopped and was standing still between two fallen logs. There was no shot opportunity. The distance was doable, but the angle was bad. It was too much of a frontal presentation— not a high percentage shot. I waited. Time passed, but the bear didn't move; nor did I. It didn't seem like a reasonable shot was going to present itself and I was fine with that. Still, I had made up my mind to shoot if everything looked good, and then it did. There was a gravel logging road at the bottom of the hill, perhaps a quarter of a mile away, but the sound of a vehicle driving below was audible to me, and also the bear. The animal rose up slightly, faced the distant sound of crackling gravel under a truck's tires, and offered a perfect shot. I came to full draw, anchored with intent, and released. The arrow disappeared into the dark forest tunnel exactly where I had aimed. There was an audible "smack" as the arrow struck and the bear jumped forward a couple of steps and then again froze. I carefully slipped my binoculars back out of a shirt pocket and raised them ever so slowly to my eyes and studied the bear. He seemed totally unaware of my presence and still didn't move. After a few moments, he took a step and then laid down. I watched intently as I assumed he was done for. I waited about five minutes and looked again. The bear was motionless. I started to move forward and the bear's head came up ever so slightly, but it wasn't looking my direction. I carefully settled in behind a bush and watched and waited. I still assumed that the animal was weak from extreme blood loss and was near the end. Still, I wanted to be sure that I didn't push it from its bed before it expired. I contemplated sneaking up a bit and shooting again, but thought that the first arrow must have done the trick for the animal to lie down so quickly after the shot. I waited again. Twenty minutes or so passed without any movement, and I again slowly raised to my feet and started to approach. The bear's head came up again, but still didn't look my way. A bit shaken, I sat back down, now devising a plan for getting another arrow into the bear. The bedded animal was less than twenty-five yards away, but provided no shot while prone behind brush and branches. I was well camouflaged, the wind was perfect, and the forest was dark and thick where we were. It was difficult to stay motionless that close to the animal, but it still seemed like the best course of action. Another ten minutes elapsed and again the bear's head came up, but this time, it also stood and moved off another twenty yards and bedded again. I thought maybe I should just back out slowly, go back to camp, and return later with Rickey, but I just couldn't leave quite yet. I watched the bear for a couple minutes, and it got up again, moved a few more yards away, and laid back down. He was far enough away then, from where he had been when I shot initially, that I figured I could sneak up and look for my arrow and blood. Perhaps that would give me a better idea of what I might expect for recovery? The idea that the hit was perfect and the animal would die in seconds was long gone from my head. I now needed to learn what I could about the hit and devise a plan accordingly. I crawled ever so slowly forward to reach the two fallen logs where the bear had been when I shot. When I reached the spot, I could still see him bedded in the distance, still unaware of my presence. I studied the broken-up bark on the forest floor that comprised the bed where the bear had first laid. There was no blood. I scanned beyond the area to where an arrow that may have passed through the animal might be. I saw nothing. I repeated the search over and over with the same results. Looking back down the slope to the still bedded bear, I thought maybe now I should slip down and shoot him again. My binoculars helped reveal what I needed to know. The bear remained totally still until a fly would apparently bother him and he would flick an ear in response. The animal was still very much alive, and I was at a loss on how best to address the situation. No ethical hunter wants to see an animal suffer from a poor hit. Neither should anyone want to risk the overall recovery by making poor choices along the way. Should I sneak up and try and shoot again or continue to wait? As I continued to process the information that I had to make a decision on the matter, I heard two birds fly down from above and land. I thought maybe they were grosbeaks but wasn't sure and glanced upwards out of curiosity. There, high in a pine tree, one of the birds was sitting on my arrow. The broadhead was buried almost completely into the tree, and the shaft was angled slightly downward. Everything that had transpired within the past hour was now becoming clear. It seemed Rickey had pushed the bear out of its day bed when he had walked by. The sleepy bear was more concerned about that, and getting back to his nap, than much anything else. My shot had apparently hit a small branch in the dark forested tunnel before reaching the bear, deflected, and stuck harmlessly in the tree above. The noise had startled the bear, but only for a moment. Unaware of my presence, he quickly went back to his business—sleeping. I looked back down the hill where he still lay, snoozing away, picked up my gear, and slipped away to leave him to it.

Oregon black bear.

RECIPES AFTER SUCCESS

If I had a good recipe for "tag soup," I would share it now. However, rather than suggest a way to sweeten an otherwise somewhat bitter morsel, I advise remembering your unsuccessful hunts with a special kind of meal. Every time you come home without filling your tag, why not take your spouse or significant other out to dinner? Make it special—a good restaurant and a memorable meal. They deserve it after you have abandoned them for some days in pursuit of your obsessions, and in so doing, they may be happier about your next planned hunting adventure (albeit they may also hope for you to fail to punch your tag again).

CHAPTER NINE

THE ELK PRAYER

Of all the North American big game animals that one can chase with some regularity, nothing excites me more than the wapiti. They are large, cunning, inhabit some of the wildest and most beautiful country in the western United States, and make for great table fare. And for me, nothing screams of autumn more than hearing the mixture of guttural grunts and high-pitched squeals of a bull elk in the distance as the sun first illuminates the golden shimmer of a patch of quaking aspen high in an alpine meadow. Elk are spectacular creatures and worthy prey for any adventurous bowman. I grew up hunting them in Oregon and Idaho and later was blessed to pursue them in several other western states as well. The thought of an upcoming hunt always gave me a boost in the months leading up to the trip. The preparation was important, not only mentally but also physically. Elk hunting is a lot of work—particularly if you are successful—and a wise hunter will work to get in shape long before they start chasing bugles. I say "chasing bugles" because that is my favorite way to hunt bull elk. Some prefer stands over wallows or water holes; some spend hours behind good binoculars glassing distant timbered real estate; and some work hard to master elk sounds and try their luck at calling to lure a bull into range. I have tried all of those, with some success, but my preference is to be deep in elk country long before morning's first light, listening for bulls bugling, and then with a mixture of racing and sneaking, try to intercept a herd moving from their feeding to bedding areas. There is always a bit of luck to this method. Hearing the elk, if they are "talking," is only the first step. Getting in front of them is frequently challenging—there can be dozens of eyes, ears, and noses working to detect you before you get close. And then there is actually getting close enough, and getting the right angle for a good bow shot. If this pans out, it generally happens by you getting and staying as close as possible to the group, and then the herd bull eventually coming by you as he moves back and forth to tend his harem. This can work well with satellite bulls too—usually younger bulls that stay close to the herd—circling and darting in and out—hopeful to cut out a cow or two without getting whipped by the herd bull. This is the part that requires luck, but even if no shot opportunity arises, you will be well rewarded after successfully completing the first steps. Watching and waiting when close to a bull elk, whether ever getting a shot or not, will have you coming back for more. All of these things frequently crossed my mind as I prepared mentally and physically for a 2012 elk hunt in a premier hunting unit in Oregon. I had been accumulating preference points for seventeen years to draw a Wenaha Unit tag, and now that I had one, my excitement was high, and my daily exercise and shooting practice routines in preparation came easy.

One part of my pre-hunt thoughts, however, was a nagging memory of the previous season. Jim Akenson and I had been hunting on the edge of the Eagle Cap Wilderness and elk were plentiful but relatively silent. Opening day reached nearly ninety degrees. Nights were warm too. The elk fed at night, bedded in deep timber at first light, and there was no sign of any rutting activity. A small storm moved in after several days and the elk activity changed. A few bulls started to talk and began to show some interest in leaving their bachelor groups and follow cows. One bull in particular became quite vocal and gave me a chance to try to locate him in an old burn that was packed with downed timber and thick regrowth. The conditions were perfect as I moved toward his location. The sun was at my back, wind in my face, and enough other elk in the herd were stumbling around as they fed that my occasional misstep on a brittle branch seemed to be unnoticed. There were perhaps a dozen animals, well spread out, and slowly feeding as they moved towards a dense jungle of vegetation to bed for the day. There were two bulls in the bunch—a small rag horn and a slightly larger branched antlered bull who frequently sounded off with squeals and full bugles. I slipped through the old burn focusing on the bull ahead while constantly watching for other elk to appear and give me away. When heads were down, I'd move forward. When heads came up, I froze. At one point, I was sure that I had been made when an old cow stood staring my direction for what seemed like an eternity. Eventually, she dropped her head back to the ground and stepped behind some cover. I inched forward again and saw the bull in front of me—perfectly broadside and well within my effective shooting range. I squinted and focused intently as I drew the string back to the corner of my mouth and released. The arrow flew perfectly, struck with a loud crack, and the area around me came alive for a few moments with elk crashing through the woods, and then all was silent.

I waited an hour and then started to follow the bull. At first, there was no blood, then a little where he had jumped over a sun-bleached fallen log. Blood was scant, and it wasn't bright red and bubbly like I hoped—just a few drops here and there. Clearly, I had not made the chest hit that I had hoped for. Elk hit through both lungs, like any creature, stay on their feet mere seconds, but elk are tenacious. With only one lung damaged, they can go for a long time, cover a great distance, and may even escape. Based on the blood sign it was obvious that I hadn't struck one lung, let alone two. In all likelihood, my arrow had struck the shoulder directly and with little penetration. My tracking job was difficult and with an uncertain outcome. What had started as an exhilarating morning drug into a painful afternoon.

Jim joined up with me for a while, and we slowly tracked the herd and wounded bull into a dense thicket where they had bedded. Amazingly, we were able to get pretty close and take a look at most of the animals before they spooked and scattered, but we never identified the bull. As the afternoon progressed, Jim returned to camp to tend to the mules, and I wandered in the general direction that the animals had fled. There was a small stream below me and my canteen, long being empty, cried for a refill. I slowly descended to the water and as I was unshouldering my pack, I saw an elk about eighty yards below me. I pulled up my binoculars and immediately identified it as my bull. We stared at each other for a few moments—kind of like a scene from an old western movie right before the final showdown. I could see a little blood on the bull's shoulder, but he had shed the arrow somewhere. The bull eventually turned and slipped into the trees out of sight. I followed until dark but never saw him again. The animal had traveled well over a mile in nine hours. I returned to camp exhausted and disheartened. I hoped the bull would heal completely. Still, I knew that any injury could result in him being easier prey for the wolves that had recently established in the area, and I couldn't help but think of various scenarios of his eventual fate. In a paradox difficult to explain, I wished the animal whose life I had just tried to end, a long and healthy future.

* * *

When the next season came around, and I prepared for my Wenaha elk hunt, I reflected often about the previous year. Along with exercising and shooting regularly, I gathered maps, talked to people who had hunted the area before, and sorted gear. I also vowed not to have a repeat of the previous year, but also realized that some things were out of my control. The only way to absolutely ensure that I did not wound a bull would be not to shoot at one at all. After years of hunting, I had a pretty good idea of what my capabilities were, the patience and restraint that were required to maximize the likelihood of a desirable outcome, and of the many things that can go wrong. Still, I wanted more. Being a spiritual person, I also prayed. I have long been a strong believer in God as the creator of all things, and that the world would be a far better place if everyone truly followed the practices and instructions of Jesus. As such, I pray regularly— about lots of things, but this prayer was a little different. I don't remember exactly when I did it in advance of the hunt, but my silent words went something like this:

"Dear Heavenly Father. Thank you for the opportunity to enjoy your creation once again this year and hunt elk. Thank you for the special privilege of being able to hunt a special place, and the physical and financial abilities to do so. I know in the time that I have to hunt, and the area that I am going, I will probably get opportunities to shoot at a bull. Please help me not to wound an animal. I ask that you guide my arrow with the force and accuracy of David's sling when he faced Goliath. Thy will be done always. I ask this in Jesus' name. Amen."

I know for a nonreligious person, such a petition probably sounds like mumbo jumbo, and even a professed believer may question whether such a prayer would tickle the ears of God. All I can say is that it was heart-felt. I looked forward to the upcoming experience greatly, really wanted to fill the freezer again, didn't care if I shot a big bull or a small bull, but really did not want to wound one. I soon forgot about the prayer until weeks later when I stood over a monster bull taken quickly and cleanly.

The season was a month-long, but I chose to hunt the last two weeks only. I was not yet retired, so the time available to me was a factor, but I felt too that the time I did have would be the best time—the weather should be cooler and the rut should also be in full swing. I drove east about five hours from Portland and parked in a wide spot along a forest road that bordered the wilderness area. I set out with a bivy bag and lightweight gear and the intention to hike in a few miles and scout. Jim Akenson was to meet me the next day with his mules in a nearby campground, and we would decide then where we would pack into (dependent on what I discovered while scouting). The afternoon was warm and flies swarmed around me as I snuck through a series of muddy wallows about a mile from the road. The sign was encouraging. Elk tracks were fresh and numerous, and some of them were very large. I continued on for another mile and the country changed. Stringers of thick timber lined steep ridges that bisected small open meadows. A small, brush-lined creek flowed in the bottom. This was great elk country! About an hour before dark, I heard my first bugle. It was close by and was answered by two different bulls in the distance. I dropped my pack and stood still in the fading light, soaking up the sounds and the surroundings, then made a hasty camp, ate some jerky and snacks, and crawled into my sleeping bag. The otherwise stillness of the starlit night was frequently broken with screams of bull elk challenging each other. It was hard to sleep.

I was up as soon as I could see well enough to consume an energy bar and dried fruit and get my gear in order. I didn't have to hike anywhere— I was in the middle of elk country without taking a step. I heard a bugle, checked the wind, grabbed my gear, and started off. Within twenty minutes, I was looking at a five-point bull across the brush-lined creek below me. He was unaware of my presence but was just out of range and in thick willows. A bull up the creek screamed, and the five-point disappeared in that direction. I started moving that way too when I heard a bull on the ridge behind me. I again checked the wind. The approach to that bull was better, so I quickly changed plans and started climbing. Half way up the slope I stopped and listened for several minutes. Nothing. I continued to climb and then heard the bull again, not above me, but moving now to my left and up the drainage. He was moving quickly and seemed agitated. Another bull, across the creek was giving strong rebuttal to the challenges, and it seemed clear the bulls were soon to meet. I dropped back down a bit and side-hilled in the direction I predicted the encounter might occur. I was right, but not quick enough. The bulls clashed and then parted before I closed the distance. I crossed the creek to follow them and went several hundred yards before spotting the creamy patch of an elk butt ahead. A cow stepped into a small clearing and then several more. I nocked an arrow and crept forward. The herd was moving slowly away from my position until it wasn't. A bull challenged from above me and to the right, and the herd bull I had been following pushed his cows back my direction and passed right in front of me. He appeared only for a moment, pausing to look toward his challenger, and that is when I drew and released. He bolted into the adjacent timber and moments later his opponent appeared below me and then turned and followed the flee-ing herd. Though I had not been moving, I was out of breath. I forced myself to take in a lungful of air and then started the internal ques-tioning. Was the shot good? It looked good, but it had all happened so fast. I saw the arrow fly straight, and the animal had not moved until after the arrow struck. I wanted to believe there was a dead bull just over the rise, but my mind reverted back to the previous year. I was using the same equipment— a fifty-four-pound Brackenbury recurve, 2020 Classic Easton arrows, and a four-blade Phantom broadhead. The range had been similar, but this was a much larger bull. What if the arrow didn't penetrate well? I approached the spot where the bull had been standing. There was no sign of hair, blood, or the arrow. I saw only torn up earth and large deeply cut tracks headed into the timber. I searched for my arrow and any sign of a hit a little behind where the bull had been standing before following up his tracks. While I didn't find anything there, the escape path was a different story. Within a few yards, there was a blood trail to dream for. Large amounts of bright red blood covered the brush a couple of feet off the ground and on both sides of the bull's trail. The tracking took no more than a minute and led to the bull's final resting spot. He had gone just over fifty yards and clearly had died in mere seconds. I approached quietly and knelt and gave thanks. The arrow had passed through both lungs of the bull and exited, never to be found. I had such experiences infrequently with deer and smaller game, but never larger animals. My prayer of thanks then was as heartfelt as the petition from weeks before.

Wenaha bull.

Seven hours later, I had the bull gutted, boned, bagged, and hung off the ground. I usually carry six meat bags, but the bull required an additional one, so I fashioned one from my shirt for the boned neck meat. It alone weighed over fifty pounds. It was turning dark by the time I left the bull, packed up, and hiked back to the road. By the time I arrived at the campground, Jim was waiting with a lantern illuminating his horse trailer—turned camp kitchen. I shared the story from the day, ate a welcome dinner, and slept long and contently. The next day I was reminded how valuable it is to have friends with mules. We worked our way to the bull by mid-morning, and the pack animals completed by lunchtime what would have taken me several days with a backpack. We left the meat with Dale Borum, a good friend who offered to do the butchering so I could go on a pack trip with Jim and the mules instead of immediately heading home. We headed off to the Eagle Cap Wilderness where Jim would chase elk and I would look for mule deer. But that is a different story.

Jim Akenson packing out the author's elk.

RECIPES AFTER SUCCESS

I have never tasted bad elk meat. Whether old or young, male or female, or even a bull in the rut, the meat is simply amazing if properly cared for. Like all game meat, the secret to this is keeping it cool, clean, and dry. It is great if you can hang it for a three to ten days (depending on temperature) to help with tenderness. The meat can be used for anything imaginable. I use it for roasts, steaks, stroganoff, stew, hamburger, and more. One of my favorite dishes is a simple roast. I like to cook it long and slow. Take a medium-sized roast (shoulder or rump) and rub with any cooking oil. Season with salt, pepper, and powdered garlic. Place on a piece of heavy-duty aluminum foil that is set in a roasting pan. Leave lots of foil sticking out to wrap around roast. Place a sliced onion around the meat and add a cup of red wine or cooking sherry and a tablespoon of Worcestershire sauce. Wrap the meat tightly with the foil so that it is well sealed. Cook for three hours at 350 degrees and let the meat rest for fifteen minutes before serving. Enjoy hot with vegetables, potatoes, and gravy, or cold on sandwiches.

CHAPTER TEN

TURKEYS, PREDATORS, AND SMALL GAME

I don't know of any rules on what makes something a "big game" animal vs. small (or even medium). The same can probably be said about "dangerous game"—since everyone knows following up a wounded grizzly bear can be hazardous to one's well-being, but so can approaching a wounded bushbuck or wild boar. The closest I have ever come to being gored by an animal I was attempting to take was by a whitetail buck, and the only time I ever was put up a tree by an aggressive animal was by a very territorial male ostrich in South Africa. All that said, there are general accepted categories of North American game, but even here, the lines sometimes get blurred, such as with wild turkeys, javelina, or mountain lion. Suffice it to say, each critter is whatever the state game regs say it is. A mountain lion may be treated as big game in Montana and still be considered an unpro-tected predator in Texas, or a wild turkey may be treated as big game in Arizona but just another game bird in Hawaii. States vary too on what is protected, treated as a furbearer (thereby likely having dif-ferent rules apply) or considered a pest. For example, coyotes can be hunted year-round in Oregon without limit, but one must have a hunting license. In Nevada, anyone can take coyotes without season or limit, and no license is required. Regardless of differing rules around the country, one thing remains the same: there is a great deal of hunting opportunity for small game and other animals throughout the year that can help keep the hunter afield, practiced, and also provide some unusual and memorable meals.

* * *

I have taken more forest grouse with a bow more than any other category of small game and routinely carry an arrow tipped with a *Judu* head or rubber blunt in my quiver primarily for this purpose when hunting other species. This arrow not only supports the opportunity to take small game without wasting a broadhead while in pursuit of deer or elk, but also can be used for practice on a rotted stump or dead stalk of grass. I highly recommend that bowhunters warm up with a shot or two when first striking out each day. I used to carry a flu flu arrow for such purposes, but have since switched to using a replica of my broadhead-tipped arrows. This helps my practice to be more meaningful and also provides a spare arrow should I need it later for big game (and I carry a separate sharpened broadhead—carefully wrapped—in my hunting pack for this purpose). I can offer no real advice on bowhunting grouse. They can be abundant, fun to chase, and a tasty addition for the camp kitchen. I do suggest avoiding trying to shoot them out of trees without being sure of where your arrow will safely land. If not, you might spend more time hunting for your arrows than your intended prey.

Of course, you can try and take grouse on the wing and I have tried, but never successfully. Wing shooting with traditional archery equipment can be a hoot and some people get really good at it. While no grouse have fallen from the air to any arrow that I have released, I have successfully taken pheasant, quail, ducks, and geese on the wing (and also that one unlucky snipe). Successful wing shooting is benefitted by lots and lots of practice and a little luck. Some might argue that special equipment can help, perhaps a light target bow and/or the use of a *Snaro* or other arrowhead that has a large surface area. I believe, however, that using the heaviest bow that you are comfortable with, and use regularly, is the best. Special wing-shooting heads seem to always fly funny and make whistling noises for me. I stick with old broadheads or *Judo* points. I think broadheads are best, but advise against them if you are using a dog to help flush and retrieve birds. One particularly fun hunt for me is hunting ducks and geese on an incoming tide along the coast. I use old cedar arrows and many of those which miss (which is most of them) are returned on a future wave.

Dogs increase the pleasure when hunting birds, but be careful using broadheads to protect your canine partner.

Rabbits and hares can be great fun to chase. They are found in many habitats—from the Arctic tundra to the Sonoran Desert.

When pursuing cottontails and jackrabbits in the high desert, I often use a back quiver and fill it with all kinds of rebuilt arrows. I fully expect to lose or break a high percentage of what I shoot and I don't like to be thinking about that when a bunny appears. One good set up is a wooden arrow that has seen better days (but has no cracks or chips) and tipped with an empty .38 Special or .357 Magnum cartridge. The empty brass are inexpensive and make remarkably good rabbit points.

Jackrabbits are fun to hunt and can be good table fare too.

Ground squirrels can be pursued with most any equipment, but when going after tree squirrels, I recommend using a flu flu arrow. Even then, shooting up into trees can result in many a lodged or otherwise lost shaft. It is the price of admission. Use a rubber blunt to avoid sticking into limbs but understand that lost and broken arrows are likely. In my experience, if you wait for a bushytail to exit a tree before taking a shot, you better have something else planned for supper.

*   *   *

There is something special about wild turkeys. At times, they can be incredibly crafty—something is trying to eat them from the moment they crack their egg and peek into the world, and they are all about trying to prevent that. At other times, they seem remarkably stupid. I have seen gobblers jump on and try and mount or peck at a nearby bird that I have just killed. They must have thought that I only had one tag, or they really, really hated the other guy. At the end of the day, however, ninety-nine out of hundred (of those days) are going to be "crafty ones" for an old tom. If not, they wouldn't be old toms.

I was bitten by the turkey hunting bug while still a wildlife student at Oregon State University. At that time, Oregon only gave 300 permits for a spring hunt: 250 tags for an area near Hood River and The Dalles, and 50 tags for northeastern Oregon. I drew one of the more plentiful permits and bought a call before driving to the unit, reading the instructions while sitting under a pine tree, having just seen what looked like a turkey turd. A thunderous gobble echoed back from down the valley after my first pull on the cedar box. My heart started pounding. I crawled under a low hanging limb and got ready. Over two hours later, the tom appeared and gave my hiding place a once over—close enough for the twelve gauge. I suspect the bird had never heard a box call before. Only thirty-some birds were taken in the State that year. As a side, Oregon has experienced quite a success story with reintroduced wild turkeys. A hunter may now take three bearded birds in the spring and two of either sex in the fall, all with over-the-counter tags.

After moving to Alaska, I found myself in the only state in the Union that didn't have a huntable wild turkey population. I traveled to hunt them when I could and took birds in Mississippi, Missouri, Texas, Arizona, California, and Hawaii. After taking quite a few birds with a shotgun, I was ready to switch to traditional archery equipment. My first real opportunity came when invited to Missouri by Rickey Davidson to hunt family property. I was set up in a primo spot that he and his family called "the killing field." They wanted me to have the best chance possible at arrowing a bird. On opening morning, I was tucked into a homemade blind, fully camouflaged from head to toe, a short recurve in my lap and two hen decoys in front of me. I heard several turkeys fly off the roost and I started calling with a few seductive clucks. Each time I called I got immediate answers: one well behind me, and two birds together, just the other side of an old barbed wire fence on the edge of a ravine, and just out of sight. The birds gobbled repeatedly, dueling with each other for a long time, and eventually the pair crossed the fence and approached my set up. As they neared my blind and decoys, they began spitting and drumming and putting on a display they were certain would draw the two hens to them. When they didn't budge (being decoys), eventually the boys came in for a closer look. I had stopped calling and was sitting low in the shadows of the blind with an arrow nocked. At just over ten yards, one of the gobblers turned away and was completed fanned out. The other was also facing away, but his tail fan was only partially extended. I drew carefully and before I could reach full draw, both toms were in the air flying back over the fence and into the ravine. I had been introduced to hunting wild turkeys with a stick bow: turkeys one, me zero.

Over the years, I wish I could say that I evened the score, but the tally today is probably something like turkeys a hundred or more; me seven. Honestly that is what makes it special. There are a variety of tricks that improve one's chances to connect with a bird, but nothing beats spending time in the turkey woods and being patient. The last bird I took came after I hunted twenty-eight mornings without connecting. Being retired, and living on land with turkeys, made the difference—a short hunt was an easy and enjoyable way to start most spring mornings.

There are a few tips I can share. First, hunt the earliest part of the season possible. The birds are usually more active and vulnerable then. You can also locate them easier before all the leaves are fully out on trees and bushes, and before insects and breeding birds get increasingly noisy as the weather warms. Don't give up after first light. While the traditional way to hunt turkeys in the spring is commonly to attempt to call them off the roost to your set up at first light, frequently the toms are with hens then. They may gobble a bunch, but often won't leave the ladies they flew down with until later in the morning. As the season progresses, hens will feed after flying down for a short period, but then sneak off to sit on a nest. This can be a good time to call in a gobbler that is roaming in search of company. Decoys and blinds can make a real difference, but I have taken just as many birds without them. Very careful still hunting and stalking in feeding areas can be productive. Finally, use a large razor-sharp multiblade broadhead that you shoot well. Don't fall for the gimmick heads that are supposed to decapitate a bird or otherwise enhance recovery. Turkeys are tough and unless shot through the heart/lung area, or the head/neck, are prone to escape. If you break a wing, the bird can run out of the country. If you break a leg, the bird can fly. I aim for the middle—right through the base of the beard on a frontal shot, for the wing joint if from the side, and right up the poop chute on a tom facing away. If you do hit one and it escapes, don't give up looking. I recovered one bird that had been shot through the lungs but went well over 150 yards. Most, however, pile up within a few feet from where hit, if shot well.

Turkeys can be challenging to hunt with a bow –
strategic hunting techniques, reasonable shooting skill,
and a little luck, will eventually produce success.

* * *

I have hunted predators with a bow only a little and have had even less success. If you think calling in a turkey and successfully taking it with a stick bow is difficult, try the same thing with a mature coyote. I have done it only once. As such, I have no real advice to share. I do find the activity enjoyable. I have seen a great deal of interesting animals up close while predator calling: foxes, bobcats, mountain lions, marten, weasels, coyotes, javelina, and bears, as well as deer, raptors, and even a coatimundi. It also is incredibly humbling. Of course, if you use dogs to hunt cougar or bobcat, you can expect high success rates. I only went on one mountain lion hunt with hounds years ago. It was great country and it was fun to watch the dogs work. We didn't get a cat, but I recognize if we had it would have been because of the dogs and not me. This makes some believe that hunting with hounds isn't really hunting. The facts are however, that the dogs really love it, are good at it, and it really is the only effective method for hunters to take mountain lions with any dependability. Well-managed seasons and quotas ensure the species can be sustained, but without the use of dogs, managing a large cat population is difficult at best.

YOU SHOOT IT – YOU EAT IT!

There was a time that any animal that was a legal target for me most likely would be targeted by me: ground squirrels, English sparrows, porcupines—you name it. Our bowhunting club gave annual awards for both small and big game and I was pretty competitive at the time, winning either or both awards in some years. By the time I left my teens, however, I cared little that a starling was worth one point and a jackrabbit three. I recognized that hunting was a legitimate tool to control some animals, and that archery had a place in such programs, but overall, I started developing an attitude that animals harvested should be utilized to the degree possible. My first challenges with this new found ethic came with carp. They had been introduced to Oregon waters years before, were destructive to native fish and wildlife habitats, had no season or bag limit, and were fun to take with bow and arrow. Unfortunately, I found them to be extremely boney and no matter how prepared, always had a hint of muddy flavor. I slowed on taking them in the spring and turned more to bullfrogs. Their take was only somewhat regulated—they too were not native and were having some detrimental impact on other species. Also, the generous meat of the frogs' hind legs did not absorb muddy flavor like "bugle-mouth bass" and I looked forward to hunting and eating them.

Some critters can be difficult to make taste good and some small game and predators fall into this category for me. Sea ducks are one example—they are just very challenging to prepare for the table in a way that excites you and your guests (in a positive way). People's tastes vary, and each hunter needs to decide what they want to pursue, and have a plan so that the packages in the freezer of less desirable game don't continue to get buried until they are finally freezer-burned and discarded.

I tried to raise my children with the same ethic that I had grown into: you shoot it—you eat it. We would hunt animals, but would also value and respect them by utilizing them fully. We got to put this in practice when my son was about ten. He had a solid fiberglass bow with about a fifteen-pound pull and a few short wooden arrows with pressed-on metal points. It was hardly a weapon by any definition, but there is really no such thing as a "toy" bow and arrow either. One day, while strolling the neighborhood, a porcupine appeared and was ambling away down the path ahead. Remington asked if he could shoot it, and he got an affirmative reply without any expectation that his dart would connect with the animal. He pulled back and arched an arrow high, and sure enough, it landed dead center on the top of the animal's head, killing it instantly. Rem was elated, and after a little celebration, the work began (have you ever skinned a porcupine with a young boy)? Well, dinner that night was porcupine stew. It wasn't half bad, but our youngest daughter was a very finicky eater. She looked at the steaming pot and asked what it was. I replied loudly "PORK" and then very softly "you pine." She ate a little.

* * *

I've worked hard to make some game palatable. One of the biggest challenges came on a late August elk hunt. Jim Akenson and I were scouting new country and had spent the morning calling and glassing. As the day warmed, we split up and explored round about ways to get back to camp. I came upon a large alpine meadow and stopped to watch before stepping out into the clearing. I noticed movement to my left and saw a badger appear. I studied it for a moment and then decided it would make a great traditional back quiver. I took careful aim and released. The arrow soared across the meadow and struck the animal squarely in the heart. I was both excited and a little sad. I had intended to shoot it, and had made an incredible shot, but it was such a striking little animal too. I was determined that it would not only become a valued quiver but also be supper that night. I carefully skinned the badger and stashed the hide in a plastic bag and buried it in a snowfield on the way back to camp. From there, I took great care in cubing and marinating the meat in wine and garlic. When dinner time came, I told Jim I would cook, and he went off to feed and water the mules. I rinsed the meat and pounded it, salt and peppered it, and dropped the chunks in a skillet of hot butter. I set the cooked meat aside and prepared some noodles and a sour cream sauce. When Jim returned, I handed him a plate and waited. He took a bite and paused, looked up, but said nothing. I then took a bite as well. It was the worst tasting thing I ever tried to eat. At best it resembled a liver-flavored rubber ball. I spit it out and opened a can of beans. Badgers will forever be safe from me on future hunts.

This badger made for a great back quiver,
but an unsavory dinner.

RECIPES AFTER SUCCESS

Unlike badger, most small game can be made edible if not desirable. Coyote may well be another notable exception; however, bobcat, mountain lion, and lynx are all quite good, and resemble pork (without the hint of pine). The secret to successful recipes for many small game animals, especially squirrels, is to cook the meat low and slow and well-seasoned. A crockpot works well. A good recipe for ducks taken in the field is to clean and pluck or skin them, then stuff them with a sliced onion and raisins and/or pieces of dried or fresh apple. Coat the outside with lard or Crisco, season appropriately, enclose in heavy-duty aluminum foil (double wrapped), and place onto a bed of coals. Turn every five minutes for twenty minutes and open carefully so as not to burn yourself.

All rabbits are edible but some are better than others. Cottontails are my first choice, followed by snowshoe hares, and then jackrabbits. The latter take a little bit of work, but one camp recipe that I like is a basic jackrabbit stew. Cut the meat into small pieces and remove all sinew and fat. Place in a skillet with a can of beef broth and a teaspoon of hot sauce. Stir and simmer slowly until the liquid has nearly all evaporated. Add the meat to a large pot or Dutch oven and add one sliced onion, two large potatoes (cut into chunks), and three large carrots (also cut into chunks). Add three cups of water, a can of corn, a can of stewed tomatoes, a half cube of butter, and a teaspoon of seasoned salt. Simmer for two hours, stirring occasionally. Serve hot over buttered biscuits.

Wild turkeys are much like their domestic cousins except with smaller breasts and much tougher legs. The meat can also be a little drier. I usually pluck jakes (young toms) and roast them just like a domestic bird—just not nearly as long. For older gobblers, I like to pre-cook the meat for use in turkey pot pies, or make turkey fingers. To prepare turkey fingers, slice the breast meat into chunks about the size of your little finger, roll in pancake flour and seasoned salt, and fry in a hot skillet with a generous amount of olive oil. The meat should be turned only once after about two minutes and should be done in two more. Place on a plate covered with a paper towel and serve hot with cranberry sauce and stuffing. See notes in a later chapter about saving the turkey leg and thigh meat to make breakfast sausage.

CHAPTER ELEVEN

BACK TO BLACKTAILS

Most longtime hunters can quickly tell you what their favorite game to pursue is. For me it is deer, specifically blacktail deer, and more specifically yet, Columbia blacktail deer. My earliest memories of hunting big game with a bow were formed while growing up in Oregon. In those days, Bear Archery's sales pitch of becoming a "two season hunter" was a significant consideration. One could start hunting for blacktails with archery tackle in late August through most of September and, if unsuccessful, could use a firearm for the same tag through much of October until early November. And if you still hadn't filled your tag, you could pick up the bow again and try for the rest of November until early December. The bag limit was one deer of either sex when using a bow; one buck with at least one forked antler if hunting with a gun. Few serious hunters did not fill their tag. Like all good things that have to come to an end, increased crowding, reduced deer numbers, and improved hunter success rates with technological advances (primarily being the sighted compound bow), led to changes that meant having to choose between using a bow or gun. This did not impact the serious bowhunting community very much, but probably did result in fewer hunters being introduced to archery over time. While mule deer hunting on the east side of the State had continued to be more restricted (including drawing permits only for bowhunting), the blacktail hunting seasons remained close to what they had been historically. The bag limit today is one buck (spikes are legal) whether hunting with a rifle or bow in their respective seasons, and tags can still be purchased over-the-counter, as long as done so before the season begins.

Columbia blacktail deer are close relatives of mule deer, but are restricted to the western portions of California, Oregon, and Washington and a little of British Columbia. They will hybridize with mule deer, and as such, animals taken from areas immediate adjacent mule deer populations may not be considered eligible for entry into record books. They differ from mule deer in size, habitat, and behavior. Blacktails tend to live in dense brush or rainforest rather than open sage-covered plains and high desert and can be much harder to locate than their long-eared cousins. Columbia blacktails also differ from the Sitka blacktails found in Alaska. They are generally larger, spookier, and again, harder to locate when hunting. In general, I consider taking a mature Columbia blacktail buck to be in the top five of North American game in difficulty. Their range, habitat, and habits are what influence my thoughts. A big exception to this is hunting a good area in the rut, and this is what the second archery season provides in the way of opportunity in Oregon. Big bucks seem to evaporate from the landscape until November rolls around, only to appear from who knows where to anywhere there is a good number of does. This can make for some very exciting hunting.

A mature Columbia blacktail buck.

My first blacktail with a bow came during a November Oregon hunt. It was not a trophy buck, but at fifteen, it was a trophy to me. I had killed a couple of bucks with a rifle since I was first eligible to hunt at age twelve and had hunted under the "two season option" for two years, but had not released an arrow at a deer. I was plenty prepared. I had upgraded my hunting equipment to a fifty-pound Bear Kodiak Hunter, and shot very well with a new set of Easton XX77 aluminum arrows. The 2018 shafts were tipped with extremely sharp Bear Razorheads. I had confidence too, but only as much as one can have without any previous success.

I had been dropped off in the morning to hunt a steep wooded area in the western foothills of the Cascade Mountains. The area was on the edge of a migration route, and the timing coincided well with the rut. A little snow persisted on the shadowy sides of the hills, left over from an earlier storm. The day was cloudy and dark. I slipped along a well-used deer trail several hundred yards above the logging road where I had been left. My dad and a neighbor were to pick me up on the same road at the end of the day. I didn't have to worry about getting back to the drop-off site, but could come off the hill anywhere and hit the road, and they would find me. Deer tracks were plentiful and many were fresh. As I crept around a blind corner in the path, I was met by a small group of deer. They went on high alert but chose to parallel me for their escape. I had already nocked an arrow and swung and released as a young buck came by. He shot forward like a rocket as the arrow struck and then he disappeared around the corner. The shot had been surreal as the arrow had disappeared into the deer only to reappear immediately as a red mark in a snow drift on the other side of the animal. I approached the site and quickly recovered my blood-soaked arrow in the snow. It was broken in half. The buck had apparently snapped it with a leg as he bolted away. I followed the trail easily around the hill only to see my buck dead a few yards away. He had succumbed in a second or two to the shot. Full of emotion, I field-dressed my prize and then drug it down to the road to await my ride. I remember the events (of over fifty years ago) like they were yesterday.

Author's first deer with a bow.

The following two years I killed bucks with the same set up. In both cases, my dad was able to witness the shot and recovery. Generally, a naysayer of the sport, Dad then picked up a bow and worked at becoming a "two season hunter." Sadly, he never mastered any accuracy, though he practiced intensely for a while. It was some years later before I realized that the problem was almost certainly that Dad was cross-dominant. He was left-handed, but his right eye was his master eye. A similar situation occurred with my son and one of my daughters. Discovering their eye dominance early on allowed for proper training. Both learned to shoot shotguns from their left shoulder, though right-handed, and Remington learned to shoot a bow left-handed as well, though instinctively he would have chosen the opposite. While Dad gave up bowhunting nearly as quickly as he took it up, he continued to support my efforts, and I would enjoy several more years of successful bowhunting for blacktails until I completed college and moved away, but I was destined to return.

After thirty years in Alaska, I spent my last five years working for the U.S. Fish and Wildlife Service in Portland, Oregon. I then retired to 120 acres of family property near Rogue River, Oregon, and it was a blacktail paradise. Being retired, and being able to walk out my door to hunt my property and adjacent BLM land, offered ample opportunity to see, study, and hunt blacktails. I watched and photographed deer behavior. I learned where they liked to hang out. And I spent countless hours sneaking through the woods, trying to avoid poison oak, and sitting in a stand watching and waiting. I was very successful in taking bucks in coming years, but admittedly, it was more from increased opportunity than any increased skill on my part. Most of the deer were taken during November. I had an unspoken agreement with my wife that I wouldn't hunt any "regulars" seen around the house. She had names for many of them, and besides, it wouldn't do to take advantage of any of the animals that had become habituated to our presence. Come November it didn't matter much. Mature bucks wandered about freely and often I would spot a new one or two each day as the rut wore on.

My favorite location to hunt was less than a mile above our barn. It was a steep, timbered patch immediately below a clearcut. A well-used game trail bisected a mixed forest of fir, pine, oak, and madrone. The path led up to a small flat and opening that was backed by thick brush that surrounded a year-round spring. It was here that I liked to spend most of my time. The spot was favored by deer all year. They could retreat to the spring area during hot summer days, bed in the thick brush, and feed in the nearby clearcut at night. It was here where I directed a State Fish and Wildlife research biologist to search for a doe that had apparently shed her GPS collar. She had been seen regularly for the previous two years but not in recent days. Even without her collar, she would have been identifiable due to her orange ear tags. I shared with the biologist that I thought she probably had been killed by a cougar—probably near the spring. Additionally, a bear had been cleaning up the cougar-killed carcasses, not leaving much to find. When the collar was found, my suspicions were confirmed. Suffice it to say, I wasn't the only hunter that liked to pursue deer in my secret spot.

While November was the time that I waited for each year with much anticipation, my archery tag was good for the early season too, so I did hunt a little then as well, but usually without any success. The weather was frequently hot, the stalking conditions abysmal, and the deer were just plain hard to find. For whatever reason that changed one September. An early storm had blown through our area bringing rain and cooler weather. This followed an extended period of triple digit temperatures and the deer came out of the woodwork. I'd never seen anything like it. The bucks were in bachelor groups of two to six animals, and they paraded around in mid-day. If I hadn't been living where I did, and had the time I did, the event probably would have come and gone without me taking notice. I did notice however, and I took advantage of it.

After witnessing the unusual buck activity the previous day, I was up early and reached my secret spot at first light. I went to my favorite vantage point and took off my daypack and settled in atop a folding stool. I laid my Nikon camera on my pack next to my bow that had an arrow nocked and ready. Frequently, nothing particularly special would happen following this routine, but sometimes it did. But in the countless times I had set up like this before, I would more often reach for the camera than the bow. Often, it would be a bird that got my attention—maybe a flicker or Stellar's jay. I enjoyed photographing everything from bears to bugs. A flock of turkeys appeared shortly after I set down my insulated mug of coffee. They weren't close so I didn't reach for the camera. An hour passed and I was impatient and was about to pack up when I saw a flicker of a tail in the brush. I then saw antlers, followed by a deer body, and then another and another. Three bucks fed out into the opening—one was young but the other two were mature animals, both sporting Pope and Young quality racks. I ever so slowly reached for my bow and slid off the stool into a kneeling position. The animals were out of range but feeding my way. The wind was still and they showed no sign that they knew I was there. I mentally reviewed the set up. Normally, my location would be great for an ambush along the game trail between the clearcut and spring area, but I wasn't sure under the current conditions that the bucks would pass by close to where I waited. Even if they continued in the same direction, it seemed unlikely they would come through the opening and by me. With no better option, however, I waited. After ten minutes or so, the deer fed a little closer and then started moving away. I caught a glimpse of one of them occasionally as they increased their distance, but I was certain that they were not going to give me a shot where I was, so I left my gear, save my bow, and slowly moved toward them. The youngest buck sensed something he didn't like, shot his head up, and stared intently in my direction. I froze. I sighed a bit of relief when he dropped his head back down, only to quickly jerk it up again. I remained motionless but figured my hunt for the day was over. Soon, however, the buck relaxed and slowly caught up with the other two. I pursued at a safe distance, scanning ahead to see if there might be a place I could get around and in front of them without being detected. In doing so, I spied another deer approaching from a brushy gully below. He was a nice buck—every bit as big as the others. He stopped when he reached the top of the ravine and turned to look at the other deer. I drew instinctively, picked a spot behind his shoulder, and released. At the arrow's impact, the buck jumped and sped away. I knew the shot was good. I retrieved my gear from back up the hill and then looked for the arrow. It was easy to find—crimson-coated and laying on some dry oak leaves. I followed the blood sign to the downed buck. There really wasn't much blood because the deer had not gone far and was moving very quickly, but the deep hoof marks in the dirt were easy to see. He lay along a rotting log, his antlers easy to spot above the grass as they reflected the morning sunlight.

September harvest.

RECIPES AFTER SUCCESS

Like many hunters I imagine, my favorite venison meal is fried backstrap. I like to save the backstraps until later in the year to enjoy (just a foolish tradition), but I also like to cook the inside tenderloins shortly after my success. Never really a fan of liver and onions, I nevertheless save the heart and liver when convenient, but also remove the inside sweet meat strips along the backbone after field dressing. I wash them and refrigerate overnight. I then slit them in the middle, but not all the way through, so they open up butterfly style. This makes for two large and tender steaks. They are great when lightly seasoned and cooked quickly on the grill, but I also like to fry them in butter in a skillet. I usually will add mushrooms and continue to sauté them until golden brown—usually several minutes after removing the meat. Then I add a little flour and a small amount of milk to what remains in the skillet and simmer and stir for another few minutes to make a small amount of gravy. Serve the meat smothered with mushrooms and a drizzle of gravy over the top and savor a fine reward from your hunt.

CHAPTER TWELVE

BROOK TROUT AND BOYHOOD TREASURE

The whole coronavirus episode interrupted my otherwise busy travel plans. I couldn't fly out of the country, and even domestic travel was a bit squirrely. I turned to more local adventures to try to stay in shape—exercising in preparation for fall hunting season had become a yearlong endeavor, and a variety of outdoor adventures made the conditioning much more enjoyable. One such trip was a planned backpack venture to a mountain lake, starting with a three-hour drive from home to the trailhead. I had been there once before, but it had been over fifty years. Dad had taken me to the lake and he knew the area well. It was famous for eastern brook trout and the fishing was best right after the ice came off in late spring. I remember it was May—sometime in the 1960s. Dad and I drove to the trailhead in an old Jeep Willy's Wagon and then hiked about an hour, reaching the lake at last light. We slept tucked beneath a rocky ledge and covered our sleeping bags with a canvas tarp to shelter us from a light rain. As soon as it was light enough to see in morning, Dad fed me some fig bars and canned fruit cocktail, got me rigged up, and positioned me on a giant fallen tree that provided a natural jetty out into the lake. From there, I dropped a hook and worm into the dark water, and within moments from the bait sinking to the bottom beneath the log, I felt a tug followed by the wild dancing of my line, and then I reeled in a brightly colored brookie. I repeated this nine times—the limit at the time was ten trout—and I proudly hauled the stringer of squirming fish back to our makeshift camp where Dad had a fire and hot cocoa waiting. After cleaning and stowing the fish for an evening meal, Dad suggested that we go for a hike to the top of the mountain across the lake. The mountain was really more of a rocky ridge with a sheer cliff that dropped hundreds of feet straight down to the forest above the lake. Later, I would learn that the lake had been formed thousands of years earlier when the rock face sheared off and dammed a spring-fed creek in the basin. Looking back on that first hike up the mountain, I didn't remember much about the route, the time required to do it, or its difficulty. I did remember, however, what we discovered on top of the mountain. We had stumbled across a whole fossilized log, partially burned at some point early in its transition process, and with notable sections of the petrified wood being opalized with a spectacular milky color. The log had weighed many hundreds of pounds and was partially buried in the surrounding hard earth. Dad and I ate lunch sitting on the treasure and then departed—returning to the lake, another campfire, and trout and pancakes for dinner.

As I prepared to return to the lake and explore the area after so many years, I studied maps and developed a mental plan of attack. I packed two days of dried food, a light camp, fishing gear, and an old rock hammer that I had obtained as a gift when in grade school, but had never used. I thought that maybe I could rediscover the petrified log and strike off some opalized portions. I knew actually finding it again would be a long shot, but it would be fun trying. And maybe I could at least catch some brook trout? Brookies were my favorite fish to catch when growing up. They fought hard, tasted good, and were beautiful to look at. They were the species of choice for stocking in high mountain lakes in Oregon in those days. As years passed, researchers reported that brook trout could decimate native frog populations in confined lake environments. That, coupled with the fact that they were native to the northeastern United States and not Oregon, eventually steered managers to more often stock rainbow trout instead. While the specific hatchery stock of the rainbows used to plant the lakes was most likely genetically different than native trout locally, at least the species was indigenous to the general area. I understood the decision but also felt the loss of something important from my youth. A few lakes and streams maintained natural reproduction of the historically stocked brook trout—where I was returning was reported to be one of them. I was anxious to find out.

The drive was unfamiliar to me, but once I reached the trailhead, I had a slight recognition of the surroundings. I shouldered my pack and grabbed my hardwood hiking staff before heading up the trail. Two young women passed me coming down. There was only one other vehicle besides mine in the parking area—I would have the area ahead to myself for at least a little while. I smiled. After a couple miles of climbing, I reached a side trail and took it to the lake. I worked my way around to a series of outcroppings and pitched my small tent. This seemed to be about the spot where Dad and I had camped over fifty years before. I put my rod together and worked my way to the lake's edge. Two things struck me immediately. One was the steady stream of tadpoles swimming in the shallows—hundreds of thousands of them it seemed. If brook trout still occupied the lake, they certainly were not negatively impacting the frog population! Second, a large log stretched far out into the lake from the shore. Could it be the same log that I had fished from previously, after all these years? I worked my way out onto the log and soon saw trout milling around below. The light-colored edging on their fins gave them away—they were brook trout. I caught a few and kept two for supper. The trout bag limit was now five, but two was all I needed. I cooked them in seasoned oil wrapped tightly in aluminum foil over the coals of a small fire. Their moist orange flesh was as much a delicacy as I remembered.

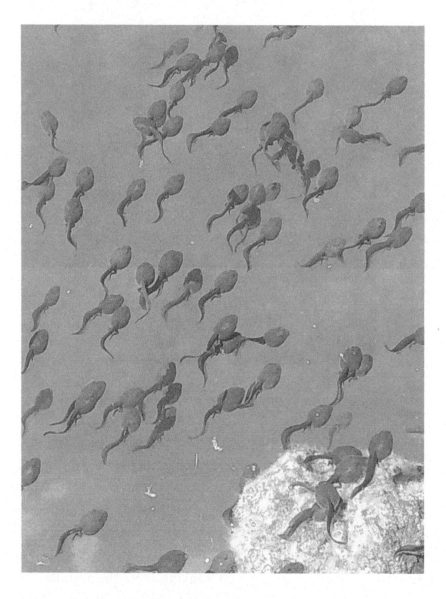

It was apparent that frogs were co-existing well with brook trout.

"Brookie" for dinner.

I laid in my sleeping bag staring upward for at least two hours before falling asleep. The fine screen of my tent kept the mosquitos away but did not significantly distort the view. Immediately following sunset, I watched the graceful flight of nighthawks swooping down over the lake—this followed by an abundance of bats diving and flitting, and finally, the emergence of one star and then another and then a thousand more. I fell asleep thinking about the next day and the possibility of rediscovering the treasure on top of the mountain.

I was up as soon as I could see without the aid of my headlamp as I wanted to complete the hike before the day warmed too much.

It was forecast to reach in the low nineties, and I wanted to be back from my climb and soaking in the lake long before such temperatures were realized. I ate some oatmeal, a granola bar, and a box of raisins—washing it down with a cup of instant coffee—then put a few things in a satchel, and headed up the mountain. The cliff face eluded me for some time. It was farther, and the approach steeper, than what I remembered. When the cliff did break into view ahead, I discovered that I had gone farther east than intended. I had planned to reach the timbered ridge and work the half-mile distance along it to the cliff, where the mountain had fractured and slipped long ago, but had gone too far. A direct ascent to the top (up the cliff face) was impossible. I studied my location and opted to try and climb up a ravine, then up a steep slope to reach a knife-edge portion of the ridge, hoping I could work my way along the backside of the ridge and to the top. To do otherwise meant aborting the effort entirely, or going back down and starting again further to the west. The restart option wasn't appealing as the day was already warm. If I started over, I would be climbing in the heat of the day. I chose the first option—to try to reach the top through very rough and increasingly steep terrain.

I enjoyed the climb, proceeding slowly and considering alternative routes with each obstacle I encountered. Wildflowers were numerous, and a humming bird, unconcerned with my presence, hovered a few feet in front of me and probed a flower with its slender bill, and then buzzed off only to reappear a few moments later and repeat its search for nectar. Soon I had climbed to where the top of the ridge was only about 250-feet above me. It was a difficult 250-feet however. The whitish earth underfoot was hard as dried cement—compacted by centuries of snow, rain, and wind. My progress slowed and advice I had frequently given others was now haunting me: "If you have to use your hands to climb up, it will be dangerous getting back down." Still, I inched my way upward. I used my walking stick to probe and push and act as a third leg of sorts. I couldn't navigate any further without it. And then I was without it. It slipped from my hand as I shifted my weight to lean more into the mountain and the staff slid in slow motion over 100-feet below before resting on a rocky ledge. I hugged the hillside even more, not immediately able to go up or down and laughed a little to myself. I had recently received an email from Kiwi friend Philip Commins who had harvested a rusa deer with his longbow in very nasty country and detailed the difficulties of recovering it (and getting himself out in one piece). I had replied to his note relaying similar predicaments that I remembered—particularly while hunting mountain goats in Alaska—but that I didn't do such crazy solo trips into rough country anymore. And yet there I was, stuck to the side of a mountain where no one knew where I was and with no cell phone coverage. I not only stared longingly downhill at my walking stick, I also started looking for options off the mountain that would minimize potential physical damage. The choices weren't good. Some routes could be disastrous; some would likely not be fatal but could result in broken bones. One route seemed a good option. It entailed a little jump and spin and then sliding down a slope and catching a small, but hopefully deeply rooted, pine tree sapling. If it worked as planned, I should be unscathed, or only have a couple minor scrapes; but if I missed catching the tree, well, not so good—the cliff and ravine lay just below. I pondered this, still leaning into the mountain and keeping my weight on the good foot hold I had, and remembered a similar predicament from years ago. Dad had wanted me on the roof at home to watch him put on new shingles. Dad was like that— he wanted his son to observe while work was being done: welding, digging, grinding, building, and car repairs. I didn't mind, though I must admit while he was very handy, I didn't inherit many of his skills. On the roof, watching Dad, I began to slip. Though I was pre-school age at the time, I remember the event well even now. The roof planks below me were not yet papered and I recall seeing a small knot hole in a board directly below me. I had no concern as I slid forward—I was going to stick a couple of fingers in that knot hole as I passed and arrest my slide before I fell over the roof's edge. As I slid towards it, I remember Dad scrambling down from the eve and scooping me up, saving me. Would my plan have worked? I thought it would at the time, but would never know. Now I formed a similar plan. Would it work?

The plan might work, but the stakes were high. I didn't like any of the choices, and I wasn't going to make the decision in haste. That said, my muscles were tiring, and I couldn't hug the hillside forever. Then it dawned on me. Inside my satchel was my old rock hammer. I pulled it out and began slowly chipping out footholds in the hard earth to facilitate a careful zig zag descent back down the mountain. I completed the work slowly and methodically, but it was effective. In about twenty minutes time, I reached my walking stick. An hour later, I was back in the forested area below and found a small spring gurgling up from a fissure in the rocks. I sat and drank cool water and gave thanks. I would not go look for the petrified log this trip, or perhaps ever. I had discovered at the trailhead that the entire area was now designated wilderness; I had already decided that chipping away at its treasures wasn't now legal, ethical, or something I needed to do. Besides, unfulfilled dreams are good to have—just as are fond memories. Sometimes an old rock hammer is good to have too.

Old rock hammer and rock hammerer.

RECIPES AFTER SUCCESS

A great way to enjoy a fresh fish dinner in the backcountry is to cook them in foil over coals. I carry about a two-foot section of heavy-duty aluminum foil folded up into a tight square in a small plastic bag, which also includes a couple of teaspoons of seasoning

(I usually stick to garlic salt). You don't need a large fire, but you do have to be patient to wait for coals to form. I gut the fish but leave the head on, sprinkle a pinch of seasoning inside, use a little oil or margarine if available (but not required) and double wrap tightly in the foil. Place on hot coals but not open flame. Once you have heard sizzling for about four minutes, flip the packet over (careful not to burn yourself or puncture the packet) and leave for about four more minutes. How long to leave depends on the heat of the fire and the size of the fish. Open carefully to expose the head. If the eyes are milky, it is done. This is a great way to supplement a freeze-dried dinner, but I never absolutely count on it. Sometimes the fish just aren't biting.

CHAPTER THIRTEEN

A TALE OF TWO BROADHEADS

Over the years of trapsing over countless miles of tundra, forest, and desert, I have occasionally found evidence of bowhunters who had hunted there before me. In fact, one of my favorite pastimes as a child was looking for arrowheads. Some of the fun came from the unique places visited when engaging in the activity and some was from the excitement of discovery. And some was from holding a newly found object in my hand and wondering about its history—was it made from local material or traded from afar, had it been used to take game, or was it used in battle? My infatuation with arrowheads and similar artifacts has not waned over the years, but my collection of them ceased long ago. Once employed as a federal land manager, and gaining an understanding of the laws associated with artifact collecting, I willingly gave up the effort. I still enjoy finding arrowheads and other vestiges of the past, and still go through the thought process of contemplating their origin, but nowadays I may photograph the object (and might even take a GPS reading) and then leave it where I found it.

ARROWHEAD COLLECTING REALITIES

Now might be a good time to stray from my story to explain the rules, as I understand them, pertaining to collecting arrowheads, as many a fellow bowhunter probably has the same fetish that I do. At a time when the United States was becoming more environmentally aware in general, having passed laws that protected everything from endangered species to marine mammals (and having already addressed issues regarding clean air and water, and environmental decision-making processes for federal projects), arguments were also being made that archeological sites and artifacts were an important and irreplaceable part of America's history and were being lost from public lands at an alarming rate. Previous laws, most notably the Antiquities Act of 1906 and National Historic Preservation Act of 1966, did not stem the increasing rate of disturbance to archeological sites or removal of artifacts—the most egregious being excavation of Native American village and burial sites. Congress debated the issue at length and ultimately passed the Archaeological Resources Protection Act (ARPA) in 1979. A hot topic in the debate leading to the final language of the law included the surface collection of arrowheads, where no digging occurred, and where no other disturbance took place, other than the pocketing of a small artifact. Ultimately, a provision was included that exempted the surface collection of arrowheads on federal public lands—this sometimes referred to as the "Jimmy Carter Clause"—probably not so much from him weighing in on the legislative language, as him being the president that signed the bill. The exception seemed to include pretty plain language; however, it really did little to protect the would-be arrowhead collector. First, most of what is found is more likely a knife, spear point, scraper, or atlatl point rather than a small projectile point meeting the definition of "arrowhead." Second, the exception only protected from the severe penalties of ARPA if an arrowhead was collected from public land, but such items are also considered "property" and cannot be taken without a permit under provisions of other laws. In other words, expect to get a fine if you collect an arrowhead, but not as large a one as if you pick up a spear point, dig up artifacts, or otherwise knowingly disturb archeological resources. Repeated and more damaging offenses can result in jail time as well as large fines.

Like all laws, we can argue that they are good or bad, should be different, or should be repealed entirely. Nonetheless, history teaches us that laws such as ARPA generally are strengthened if anything over time. Most states now have similar laws as the federal rules and require permits for collection of artifacts, as well as penalty provisions to address violations. Some exceptions are found in some states (and for some types of artifacts, such as arrowheads) on private property; however, one should be well versed in the local laws before pocketing any artifact. This even includes the debitage (flakes and chips) found at ancient tool-making sites.

Obsidian arrowhead of unknown origin –
appreciated and left where found.

* * *

So now, on to my story. Inevitably modern bowhunters lose arrows just like their ancient brethren, and parts that remain are often discovered by others in years to follow. Like when discovering an obsidian or flint point, I go through a similar thought process when finding a modern arrowhead—posing the questions to myself of where it came from, who lost it, and had it successfully taken game? On a post-retirement elk bowhunting trip to northeast Oregon, I got to ask these questions twice during the three weeks I roamed the hills there. The first discovery was a three-blade broadhead affixed to a short piece of a fiberglass shaft which I noticed buried in the dirt aside a well-used game trail. It had been there a long time, and there was not much I could surmise about its history. Given that only a couple of inches of shaft remained, I guessed that the arrow had probably been embedded in antler or bone and broke off as the animal fled, but I would never know. The second arrowhead was found a week or more later and many miles away from the first. This one came with some less guesswork. While I would probably never learn who the hunter was that launched the aluminum shaft and four-blade head, the timeframe and intended target were certain. The broken shaft and head were inside the bleached ribcage of a five-point bull elk, shot and not recovered the previous season. I tried not to judge, not knowing the circumstances, for I have occasionally lost game too. It happens to anyone who hunts long enough. Still, the hit appeared to have been in the lung area, and the shaft was broken in a place to suggest more than adequate penetration. Then again, the skeleton was in a brushy creek bottom—the kind of place a wounded bull would seek out over time, but not necessarily where a mortally shot bull would end if it succumbed to its wound quickly. Like with the first broadhead, however, much of the history of the second would also remain a mystery.

I kept both of the broken arrows that I discovered, and when I got home, I removed the heads and set them aside, forming an idea that I would try to reuse them on future hunts to take game—a sort of recycling for sure, but also maybe to perpetuate their memory, and honor their original unknown users. I chose two species that I am very fond of hunting for the endeavor: turkey and javelina. These are critters that are abundant, have long seasons, are good to eat, and increasingly important, as I age, easy to pack!

BROADHEAD ONE – TURKEY QUEST

The first quest came together rather quickly. After the early fall deer and elk season in Oregon, I acquired a new Liberty long-bow from Allen Boice in Roseburg. I had struggled to shoot my six-ty-pound Hill-style longbow as accurately as I liked and decided to downsize to fifty-five-pounds. The new bow shot extremely well for me and with minimal practice I was able to shoot under four-inch groups at twenty-five yards with near certainty.

Fall turkey hunting is much different than that in the spring. The gobblers are pretty quiet and don't respond to a call well. On the other hand, the season is long, allows the take of either sex birds, and also includes newly hatched birds, which are generally near full grown but can be more naïve and easier to approach. I say naïve in a relative way. All wild turkeys from the day they hatch until the day they swallow their last acorn or bug are pretty alert. If they weren't, a coyote or hawk would make short work of them.

Recycled broadhead number one.

While spring turkey hunting may entail a regular routine of attempting to call birds to a blind and decoy, often right off the roost at first light, fall hunting can include more variety, such as spot and stalk, ambush, or breaking up a flock and trying to call scattered birds back to your location. As such, hunting in the fall can be more like hunting other game—covering lots of country until birds are located and then figuring out a strategy of how to get within bow range. While maybe not the most productive, my favorite technique nonetheless is to walk rapidly through the woods until I see fresh turkey sign and then slow my pace, or until I see birds at a distance, and then plan a slow stalk into my effective range. The birds have incredible eyesight and very good hearing, but fortunately, they have a very poor sense of smell, so paying attention to the wind direction isn't necessary. This can prove to be a big advantage when stalking turkeys as use of cover becomes the primary concern, and sneaking from bush to tree without worrying about where your scent is going is huge. On cool fall days, turkeys spend most of their time moving slowly and feeding—scratching in the forest litter and pecking at potential morsels. They may also have a bit of a false sense of security being in a flock; however, that only helps when they are engrossed in working a particularly good food source and none of the birds are alert. Such conditions existed in my early November Oregon hunt. I spotted a group of seven or eight turkeys feeding in tall grass— apparently stripping the seedheads and then pecking at them on the ground. The grass was tall enough that the birds were out of sight unless one popped up its head, which they did irregularly, like a periscope being extended to check for potential danger. I was lucky that no heads popped up while I made my approach. I think if I am honest, I would have to say there is always some degree of luck when I fill a turkey tag with traditional archery equipment outside of a blind, and sometimes even then. With an arrow nocked, I froze in a stooped position when about twenty yards from the birds. A head popped up, and then two, but they quickly went back down and I drew to full draw and released through the grass at the mid-section of a yearling tom. The three-blade recycled head broke a wing bone at its base as it entered the turkey, stuck into the ground on the far side, pinning the bird momentarily. The rest of the flock took wing, but the arrowed tom flopped in place for only a moment and then was still. The first part of my goal was completed after only three hours of hunting.

Success with first recycled broadhead.

BROADHEAD TWO – JAVELINA

The second goal would be much more drawn out to achieve. In theory, javelina are much easier to harvest with traditional archery equipment than wild turkeys; however, other factors contributed to a lengthy delay in accomplishing the second part of my quest.

I had planned to try for javelina a couple months after the turkey hunt, but woke up one morning with my right shoulder very stiff and sore. I had spent a few weeks working hard on our property—splitting wood, pulling old fence posts, and cutting up and hauling off heavy pieces of metal from deteriorating gates and culverts. I thought that the shoulder would feel better after some Advil and a day or two of rest. It didn't. By the time I got in to see my doctor, the shoulder had totally locked up. I couldn't raise my arm above my waist, and the pain was bad enough that sleep was difficult. The doc diagnosed my condition as adhesive capsulitis, or "frozen shoulder." I would learn that the condition was quite common—the body's way of protecting a joint that is being overused—but I didn't recall hearing of the term until it first rolled off the doctor's lips. I did daily exercises, saw a physical therapist three times a week, and received the usual cortisone shots and other treatments, but I couldn't pull a bow of any kind for over a year and a half. It was another year of working with a fifteen-pound youth bow before I could shoot anything of a weight that I might ethically hunt larger animals with. I visited Allen Boice again, and this time bought a forty-pound two-piece Liberty longbow. Though legal, this was still too light for deer and elk in my mind, but fine for javelina. After over two years of delay, I was off to Arizona to chase javelina.

Recycled broadhead number two.

The second recycled broadhead was a fixed four-blade weighing 125 grains. It flew well on the tiny Easton 1816 shafts I had been using with the new bow, but my effective range was only about fifteen yards, largely due to limited practice—even the forty-pound draw was still challenging to my recovering shoulder. Because of this, my opportunities to take a javelina were limited. I made stalks on several animals during my ten-day hunt, but I could never get close enough before being seen or winded. On the last evening of the hunt, I shot a cottontail rabbit at twelve yards with the recycled head. I wanted a confidence builder, and got it. The arrow killed the rabbit instantly, and I skinned it and took it back to camp to roast over a mesquite fire. Unfortunately, the arrow buried in matted grass after exiting the rabbit, and I was unable to recover it in the fading light. Perhaps someone would find it in coming years as I had? At this point, however, while wandering the Sonoran Desert, I had also found two new arrows with three-blade heads that had been lost very recently by someone else. It looked to me that a bowhunter may have been following javelina down a dry wash, emptying their quiver as they went, not returning to look for the spent arrows. I vied to return the next year and complete the quest—albeit with two newly recycled broadheads.

The following January found me back in Arizona. My shoulder was nearly healed and I was shooting a fifty-pound Meigs longbow well out to thirty yards. My confidence was high. I was having difficulty finding javelina however. While their home range is relatively small, javelina may change food selection and primary habitat use somewhat from year to year. Simply put, they were not to be found in the prickly pear covered rolling hills like the previous season. After several days of hunting, I relocated to flatter terrain and found plenty of fresh sign where javelina had been digging holes while searching for succulent roots. I sat on a distant knoll to glass the surrounding area near where I had found the fresh diggings. Late on the fourth day, I spied a group of eight javelina rooting in a wide-open area about 500 yards away. Since there was essentially no cover, I waited until last shooting light to close the final distance for a shot. A large boar was off to the right from the rest of the herd and I focused on him. I closed to within thirty yards as the animal dug and rooted and I then waited for the right angle to present itself. When he turned broadside, I drew and released. The arrow looked perfect—disappearing into the peccary low and tight behind the shoulder. He grunted loudly and took off on a quick trot across the open desert and towards a brushy draw. Javelina are not tough. If hit well they don't go far—sometimes only mere feet before expiring. This guy was running full out, and it was immediately clear that the shot was not as good as I had thought. I followed quickly, easily following the tracks that dug deeply into the sandy earth as I scanned the area ahead. There was no blood. The boar was carrying the arrow, but it hadn't hit anything vital. I reached the brushy thicket that lined the wash and saw where the animal had stopped momentarily and then had taken off again. Still there was no blood. There also was no more daylight. I returned to camp using my flashlight and spent a long restless night in my sleeping bag wondering where the arrow had hit and where the boar had gone. I returned the next morning to the spot where I had stopped tracking the evening before, and at first, the tracks were still easy to follow. Eventually however, the boar left the sandy wash and started crossing open hardpan desert. Soon I was only guessing where he had gone and after several hours the search was more of wandering widely from one patch of cover to the next. I did not find the javelina or the arrow. I spent another day and a half in similar fashion, but my search was in vain. I broke camp to pick up my wife at the Tucson airport but was set to return after a planned week of touring southern Arizona.

Eight days after I had shot the javelina, I returned to the area and pitched my tent after dark. The next morning, I hiked to the top of my glassing knoll thirty minutes before sunrise and hunkered down, waiting for enough daylight to use my binoculars. The sun slowly slipped over the horizon and gradually illuminated the valley below. I heard a coyote howl in the distance and studied the area from whence the sound had come—spying one and then a second animal loping across an opening below. I glassed close, then out a few hundred yards, and then out to a half mile or more, only spying a small mule deer buck working its way toward some distant rimrock. No javelina were seen. As the sun warmed my body, I glanced down at my bow and quiver. The outside arrow in the quiver was tipped with the remaining recovered broadhead—the second found from the previous year's hunt. I daydreamed a bit and relived the discovery and use of all the broadheads—the first two being found on an elk hunt and being used to take a turkey and rabbit. The second two being found on an earlier javelina hunt of which one was carried off in the area below me a little over a week earlier. I studied the remaining head and considered what its fate might be. Eventually, I picked up my gear and started down the slope and out into the desert, intent on still-hunting along the brushy edge of the wash below until the heat of the day would incentivize me to return to camp for lunch and a siesta. I had been sneaking along no more than an hour when I glanced back toward the knoll and spied some movement. I raised my binoculars and quickly identified a lone javelina feeding near where I had been just a short time before. I rounded the knoll to approach the top, with the morning breeze in my face. Fortunately, the sun was also on my back—perfect stalking conditions. At first, when I neared the place where the peccary was last seen, I saw nothing and I feared that somehow it had been alerted to my approach. Patience prevailed however—after nearly ten minutes of standing still and scanning the area ahead, the boar reappeared no more than thirty-five yards away. I crept closer as the animal was intent in its digging. At eighteen yards, I drew and released. The arrow found its mark and the boar ran a few yards downhill and rolled on its side. It kicked a couple times and then was still.

The last recycled broadhead had found had penetrated both lungs and death came quickly. I approached the downed animal and took off my pack and gave thanks as I sat. I then enjoyed a snack and reminisced again about the multi-year quest to use the two recycled broadheads—two that ultimately turned into four. I gutted the animal and put it into a large game bag to carry back to camp where my tent was pitched next to a large paloverde tree—perfect for hanging the boar and skinning it in the shade When I was in the middle of the task—pulling the hide down over the shoulders of the animal, I made a surprising discovery. A three-blade broadhead mark was clearly evident in the lower brisket area—penetrating the skin on both sides and about an inch deep in muscle. This was the same animal I had struck eight days earlier! I again gave thanks and then chuckled to myself. I now knew the fate of the animal I had hit. The arrow it carried off, however, was another matter. Perhaps it would be discovered by another hunter in years to come; perhaps even reused to create a new memory?

Quest completed.

RECIPES AFTER SUCCESS

Counter to what some may say, both wild turkeys and javelina are very good to eat. I have tried lots of recipes, and some are better than others, but the two I share here both include hickory-smoked bacon, so you know you can't go wrong (everything tastes better with bacon)!

I like to make breakfast sausage from wild turkey. I generally limit this to using dark meat from two or three birds that I have frozen until I have enough to make a batch. Some folks discard leg and thigh meat from game birds they harvest, but that is a lot of waste, particularly from a turkey. You can add breast meat if you choose, but I generally use this for other dishes, such as in a pot pie or for fried "fingers." You can also use meat from other birds. I have used grouse and pheasant legs and thighs to supplement my sausage-making on occasion. Remove any gristle or bone from the leg and thigh meat and coarse grind equal amounts of bird and quality bacon. Season with red pepper, garlic salt, onion powder, chili powder, and any other seasoning that sounds good to you. Mix thoroughly and freeze double wrapped in about one-pound packages. I use freezer zip-lock bags and then freezer paper. With this method, I have found that the meat is still fresh tasting even after two or three years in the freezer. Thaw when ready to use and make patties to pan fry for breakfast, or meat balls to serve with barbecue sauce as an appetizer.

For years, I barbecued javelina meat, which was fine, but honestly, it wasn't as though I looked forward to the meal. I now make the entire animal into chili meat, and I have to use restraint so as not to make a pig of myself when consuming it. It is always important to handle game meat carefully to ensure quality, and this is especially important with javelina. They have scent glands that produce a musky secretion. It is important to remember that you should never touch the hide and then the meat during the gutting and skinning process. I like to hang the animal if possible and wear surgical gloves when cleaning it. A little extra effort on the front end will pay dividends at the table later. Like with the turkey legs and thighs, I cube the cleaned javelina meat and then grind it with quality bacon, but I use an approximate 25 percent bacon and 75 percent javelina meat mix versus 50–50 for turkey sausage. Freeze in one- to two-pound packages until ready to use. Thaw and brown the meat in a lightly oiled skillet. Drain any excess moisture once browned and then stir in one 1.25-oz chili seasoning packet (available at most grocery stores in the gravy mix section). In a separate saucepan, bring to a low boil two 15.5-oz cans of dark red kidney beans and two 14.5-oz cans of diced tomatoes. I like one of these to include green chiles. Add the browned and seasoned meat to the beans and tomatoes and reduce the heat. Let simmer for at least twenty minutes, stirring occasionally, and serve over fresh cornbread with some grated cheese on top.

CHAPTER FOURTEEN

RETURN TO THE CHURCH

Everyone who travels and hunts repeatedly over the years is likely to develop a short list of special places that have created exceptional memories—places they hope to revisit again and again, and with hopes too that these places remain as they were before, wild and beautiful and full of game. I have a short list of such areas. Some of them I used to call my "A" places—areas like Alaska, Arizona and Africa—places whose names started and ended in the letter "A." I realized however, that there were lots of "A" places that I had never visited (like Albania and Algeria) and others that I had visited but not hunted (like Alabama and Australia) and that the label was pretty foolish. Besides, my "A" places were entire states and a continent, not really distinct pieces of real estate, and that I had visited many special places too that didn't start or end with an "A." When I pondered the subject at length, one "non-A" A place stood out more than any other: the Frank Church—River of No Return Wilderness in central Idaho (hereafter referred to as "the Church").

Growing up in rural Oregon, my family had plenty of opportunities to hunt deer and elk, and we were generally successful too. A good advertisement for our home might have included a jingle like, "Venison; it's what's for dinner." I can count on one hand how many times I remember eating beef in our house. It just wasn't done and it wasn't necessary. But because we were a hunting family, we looked beyond Oregon's borders to even better opportunities to find wild country and abundant game, and central Idaho was less than a two-day drive from our home.

Dad was first invited to explore the area around Big Creek in the late 1960s with a group of loggers he worked with in southern Oregon. After a couple of trips, he ventured off on his own—wanting to discover new country and not burden his hosts that had shown him the ropes initially. The area was not yet protected as wilderness and people drove every kind of four-wheel drive rig imaginable into the backcountry. Still, one had to have pack stock to realize the full potential of the area and to help pack out game once successful. Dad's mentors had all used horses, to ride and pack. For some reason Dad opted to build a pack-string of donkeys. I suspect it was for cost reasons (purchase price, gear, feed, maintenance, and transportation), but the choice proved wise. We were able to access country the horse people couldn't or wouldn't use. We started small—little pack burros like those prospectors tugged around the desert, but gradually we worked up to a string of "mammoth jacks." Packing a bull elk out with the smaller stock took three animals; with the mammoth jacks only two were required.

Wayne West packing out of the Church.
Photo by Ralph Milton

My first trip to the Church was in 1971. Policy changes were in the wind that would lead to a study of the Idaho Primitive Area (for potential inclusion in the National Wilderness System), but in that year, no vehicle restrictions had yet been put in place, and it showed. Trucks and trailers filled the mining road paralleling the creek from Big Creek Ranger Station to Monumental Bar, where people then tried to turn around, or find a place to park to begin their adventure. From there, people could venture off in three directions: head toward Chamberlain Basin, down Big Creek, or up Monumental Creek. Each route had countless miles of main and side pack trails—plenty of area to absorb the swarm of hunters, but the access road and parking area created a huge bottleneck. Still, most travelers were patient and friendly. Active pack-strings were given the right-of-way and folks worked together when meeting head on while driving trucks and trailers with no place to pass either direction for a mile or more. One of my most vivid memories of the drive along Big Creek was the pole bridges. Some rigs just forded the streams rather than cross on the bridges, but they seemed sturdy enough: several layers of crisscrossed lodgepoles and planks spanning the creeks. While some drivers opted to cross the makeshift spans, most pack animals did not—much preferring to wade over slippery rocks than dance across rickety poles. When it was all done, I am sure it would have been quicker to walk from Big Creek Ranger Station to Monumental Bar, but that wasn't how it was done then.

Having donkeys meant that we walked with them rather than ride them. They were too valuable carrying gear to be carrying us, and their pace was slow enough that we could keep up. We averaged three miles per hour so most trips to our base camp (about twenty-one miles in) took more than a day. The trip in 1971 opened my eyes to multi-day travel to reach a hunting destination. It also brought home the realization of what truly great country existed, if one was willing to work to access it. On that trip, we took two large bull elk, a mule deer buck, and a mountain goat. The donkeys earned their grain.

Crossing Big Creek.

The remote and wild nature of the area had earned a reputation, and soon after a former study area was designated, the U.S. Forest Service started managing the area to protect wilderness values while Congress took time to decide the area's fate. Miners still had limited access to valid claims, but the general public was no longer allowed to drive more than a couple miles past the ranger station.

Within a few seasons, the road became a trail, and in some places not a very good one. For those familiar with the history of the area, this phenomenon was nothing new. During the peak gold mining days in the nineteenth century, there were two trails throughout much of the route along Big Creek: one for upstream mule traffic and one for down. Mules brought everything from small household goods to complete (disassembled) stamp mills to process gold ore. There isn't much of this historic trail system visible today without significant imagination. The country is steep, rough, and both well-timbered and extremely rocky. Nature reclaims routes quickly with rock slides, floods, and burns. This is the way of the Church.

While some bemoaned the lack of access with the study area restrictions, we loved it. We weren't afraid to walk and no longer had the frustrations of unplanned meetings of vehicles on narrow blind corners or driving many hours only to find no place to park. The Church was officially protected as wilderness in 1980 (and renamed after U.S. Senator Frank Church in 1984).

I don't remember how many trips I have taken into the Church. They have joyfully started to blend together. I can piece back memories of my first few elk taken there, but that isn't important really. Overall, I once calculated that we had taken nearly forty elk in total on trips there. We also hunted, or helped others hunt, for deer, bear, moose, sheep, and goat. I hunted with bow, handgun, rifle, and camera on various trips. In the early years, Dad didn't approve of me taking my bow, and I honored his wishes. In some ways, it didn't make much difference. The seasons and bag limits were the same regardless of weapon, and much of the game had probably never seen a hunter. I recall one 6 × 6 bull elk I shot at eight yards with a .375 Weatherby. It was totally unaware of my presence and could have been collected with any weapon I imagine. In later years, my weapon of choice was most often a traditional bow. That doesn't really matter either I guess, but there seems to me just a little bit of respect offered to the Church when it gives up one of its creatures in the way of the Sheepeater Indians, who hunted the area over hundreds if not thousands of years—close, and in relative silence.

The Church stands at 2.367 million acres—the largest contiguous wilderness area outside of Alaska. In 1971, a hunter could take two deer of either sex and one elk (bull or cow) from September 18 to December 12. A nonresident license cost $135. Cutthroat trout could be kept and eaten. The year before (1970), bighorn sheep could be hunted without a drawing permit. Today, a quota system limits nonresident tags significantly, fishing for trout is catch and release, and the odds of drawing a bighorn sheep tag are a dismal 0.6 percent. Other changes have occurred. The handful of colorful characters that lived on homesteads deep within the backcountry are gone. A few inholdings still exist, but most are equipped with modern conveniences, and the people who stay there are generally affluent, not the trappers and miners that eked out a living growing vegetables and putting up enough meat and firewood to survive long and lonely winters. Still, the land itself is largely untouched. The opportunities to hunt and fish and explore still exist. And to me, the most important part of the changes brought to the Church over time is that fundamentally it hasn't changed at all. It is still wild and rugged and produces game, some of which will live a full life and die without ever seeing a human. That makes the Church truly an "A" place.

* * *

One particularly memorable trip I took to the Church occurred in the mid-1980s. Dad had drawn a bighorn sheep tag and I flew down from Alaska to join him for a couple of weeks. He left the donkeys at home. Instead, he met me in Boise, and we drove to McCall and chartered a bush plane to land on one of the few unimproved airstrips still useable after the wilderness designation. He had scouted much of the summer via backpack and now had supplies for five weeks. I only had two weeks of vacation time so would fly out early if Dad hadn't connected by then, but he was planning on staying for the duration if need be.

This was a time before cell phones and satellite GPS technology. Communication to arrange a charter pick up flight either occurred prior to, or at the time of being dropped off, or by accessing a back-country radio later in the trip. It was this option, using the radio at Taylor Ranch, that is the central to this particular tale. There were two sheep seasons for the unit and Dad had a tag for the second. We flew in a few days early and set up a base camp at Soldier Bar. There, we met a fellow sheep hunter that had been hunting the first season. He had many stories to tell, but no sheep. What he did have was a dead five-point bull elk that his seventy-year-old father had just shot, and it was hanging over four miles from the airstrip. Dad and I volunteered to help pack the meat. We needed the exercise and they needed the help. Besides, we were hoping to learn a few secrets that we might apply to our upcoming efforts to find a ram. We struck off at first light the following morning and reached the kill site in time for an early lunch. We then boned and bagged the meat and took off with heavy packs down the mountain, to stop by Taylor Ranch on the way back and radio for a plane. The ranch, a unique inholding deep within the Church, was owned by the University of Idaho and was operated as a field station for research and other academic endeavors. As we approached the ranch, we were greeted by the friendly bark of a golden retriever and then a smile and hello from Jim and Holly Akenson. The dog soon left us to return to a vigil a short distance away—a black bear had been raiding a fruit tree and had retreated up a large pine at the urging of the dog—apparently waiting until dark to retreat, or more likely, to go back for more fruit. We unshouldered our loads and settled in on the front porch while Holly brought us cold drinks and Jim worked the radio. After a while, the conversation shifted beyond the immediately obvious (we were hunters wanting to use the radio) to a little more detail about each of our lives. Jim and Holly, along with dog, horse, and multiple mules, lived at the ranch and worked as its managers for the University. Both wildlife biologists, they worked with students and on various research projects, in addition to keeping the place maintained. Their chosen lifestyle was unusual and challenging, but undeniably rewarding too. Soon our conversation transitioned to where we were all from and about hunting. Jim, Holly, and I were the same age and, come to find out, had been in the same biology class at Eastern Oregon State University in LaGrande, Oregon. Though we didn't know each other at the time, Jim and I did seem to remember each other's vehicle occasionally parked in OUR secret parking place to hunt pheasants in Ladd Marsh. We had been a lot of the same places, knew a lot of the same people, and enjoyed a lot of the same things. Most important at the time, we both lived to bow hunt, and both shot recurve bows made by Jim Brackenbury. Though approaching darkness necessitated reshouldering our burdens and heading down the trail, a life-long friendship ensued. For years to come, and to this day, Jim and I (and a growing number of like-minded friends) have gotten together to chase game, in Idaho, Alaska, Oregon, and New Zealand.

Dad was unsuccessful in finding a legal ram in the two weeks that I was able to join him, but we had a great time. We saw young rams and ewes, and plenty of other game; camped at remote high-country springs that had almost certainly been visited by sheep hunters for many years before; and sat under starlit skies that were hypnotic. All nights weren't clear however. On one particularly dark and stormy night, our teepee tent that we were sleeping in was tumbled by a mountain lion when it tripped on a taunt line while sneaking by. We were camped on a ridgetop game trail—the only flat space around. The cat was probably as surprised as we were.

Dad did eventually get his sheep. It was late in the season, and he had covered much of the large and rugged game management unit in his search for a month. He was alone when he got his ram, but the elation still showed in his diary notes that I read years later. When he stopped by Taylor Ranch to use the radio at the end of his hunt, Jim did him one better. He made the call and then saddled a mule and packed Dad's ram back to the airstrip. Dad loved Idaho and had many great adventures there, but I am certain this trip was his favorite. He was alone in the wilderness long enough to be a small part of it, and that is a lasting and special thing.

* * *

Over the years, the hunting focus for me in the Church shifted more from elk to mule deer. Dad had passed away, me living in Alaska close to moose and caribou made it difficult to justify hunting elk out-of-state to fill the freezer, and the country had changed. Large fires created new growth and food for ungulates had benefitted both deer and elk, but wolves, reintroduced in Yellowstone National Park and Central Idaho in 1995 and 1996, impacted hunting opportunities. Their numbers flourished and the game suffered. Moose numbers plummeted and elk often moved to tougher habitat to escape predation and their survival rates also dropped, but mule deer seemed to do okay. That, partnered with Jim and Holly moving back to Taylor Ranch after a few years away, provided ample incentive to visit. Bucks were rutting in November, and this provided new opportunities to see older animals that could be difficult to find earlier in the season. It also was a time when much of Alaska's hunting was done for the year, and the November weather was also more conducive for keeping meat than hunting earlier in the year—lots of reasons to justify flying into the backcountry and stringing up a bow! Not that many reasons were needed. Any time spent in the Church was easily justified in my book, but late fall was another especially memorable time of year there. The shimmering golden aspens of September were replaced with snow-capped peaks, and the shrill whistle of bull elk by the thundering crashes of bighorn rams abusing each other.

Jim Akenson and a great buck taken from the Church.
Photo by Philip Commins

* * *

It was early September 2020. I was on a ridgetop in the Imnaha Unit of northeastern Oregon gazing towards Idaho. The valley below was choked with smoke. I steadied my bow against a weathered pine and reached into my pack to get my cell phone. From past experience, I knew I could get a signal there, and I would hike to the escarpment every few days to check messages. Usually, I preferred not to turn my phone on at all during a hunt, but this year was different. The West was ablaze. Dozens of large fires, fueled by extremely hot, dry, and windy conditions were sweeping across Oregon, Idaho, Washington, and California. Hanley Jenkins had hiked into camp the previous day and said that the small towns of Talent and Phoenix in southern Oregon had all but been destroyed. That's where I lived (southern Oregon), and my wife and I were living on 120 acres of forest land, and I hadn't been able to reach her in nearly a week. I turned on the phone, saw I had one bar of signal, and sent a text. No response. I sent messages to neighbors and my sister (who lived in Grants Pass). She responded and said she would check on Shannon. A few minutes later, she let me know that all was well at our place. Something was messed up with cell coverage, but not to worry. I returned to camp and made plans to pack out the next day. I was relieved, but still, it was a tinderbox everywhere it seemed. I should be home. The twelve-hour drive was smokey—all of it. Some of the worst air conditions were actually in Portland and the northern Willamette Valley. I made it home and saw the extreme damage from the Almeda Fire that had struck our area. We were lucky. Others weren't.

Mid-September approached, and the weather changed slightly. I was anxious to get back out into the woods. While archery elk season was still open in Oregon, I also had a deer tag for Idaho and had been planning a solo backpacking trip into the Church. This was likely to be my last venture into an area that had created so many wonderful memories. I knew it would be nostalgic—I would be hunting, but that really wasn't the primary incentive for the trip.

Central Idaho had not escaped the onslaught of fires either, and I had to check carefully to ensure the area was open to access. It was—barely. A large fire near Big Creek necessitated road and trail closures for the first section of my route, but the closures bordered the trail that I would start on—they did not include it. I packed my gear and drove east from my home, fully expecting to spend the night somewhere along the road, but found myself still driving until arriving at the trailhead a few hours before daybreak. I put the seat back as far as it would go in my Subaru and pulled my sleeping bag out of its stuff sack and draped it around me. I slept, or sort of, for an hour or two and then locked the car, put on my pack, and started up the trail in the dark. As the sun gradually illuminated the trail in front of me, I smiled. Adventure lay ahead. I had a week planned to backpack fifty or more miles, revisit places that had created so many fond memories, and my schedule was mine. I would rest when tired, eat when hungry, and hunt whenever it seemed right.

The deer tag didn't create much weight in my pack. I knew that if I harvested a deer that would change drastically. I had no mis-understandings about that. Miles in, and without Jim's mules, pack-ing out a deer by myself would be a chore. If successful, I had two choices: shuttle out the meat or dry it. Over the years, I had done both. Once, in 1979, I made a whole bull elk into jerky while in the Church. The hot weather and remoteness left me little choice. The dried meat turned out fine; however, it was far too much to use by any one person under normal circumstances. I ate dried elk for over five years. Over time, to make the jerky more palatable (therefore easier to use up), I changed the recipe to add flavor: a little liquid smoke and minced garlic mixed into the brine, along with salt (but not too much), pepper, and onion powder. Patience is the key. All the meat must be cut into very thin strips, soaked in a brine overnight (I use a plastic tarp sunk in a depression dug in soft dirt or sand), padded dry, if possible, and strung over a warm but not hot, smoky fire. On this trip, along with my spice mix and fire-making materi-als, I carried a filet knife, spool of thin stainless-steel wire, parachute cord, and two small space blankets. All the gear only weighed a cou-ple of pounds, but when used properly, over several days' time, it could render seventy-five pounds of meat to less than twenty. I knew that tending the fire could be tedious. I would look for dry alder, but would supplement with anything that wasn't from an evergreen tree.

Hot windy afternoons would speed the process—if it was cool and rainy, more care would be necessary to keep the inside of the space blanket "tent" over the fire warm enough. I was ready to jerk deer meat if successful, but wouldn't really know how well it would go until I started. It was all part of the adventure.

Each step along the trail beside Big Creek brought back some memories. Old camp sites were recognized, stream crossings brought back recollection of cool drinks on hot days and wet boots on all days. Historically, game was frequently not seen to any large degree until well off the trail, but black bears were often the exception, and that was true on this trip as well. I saw one or two a day. Idaho allows you to use your deer tag on a bear (or wolf or cougar) if you choose, but I didn't have any interest in spending a lot of time making bear jerky, so I watched them and let them go. Some were spooky and took off quickly at our encounter—others would stare me down, giving me the "big eye" as if to ask, "What do you think you are doing here bud"? While the general deer and elk season had recently opened, there was only sign of one traveler ahead with a horse and mule. I had the immediate area to myself. Later in the trip, I saw one other person: on the fifth day, I had a lone hunter walk by me while leading several llamas. I said hello, but he didn't look up. Either he didn't hear me or didn't want to acknowledge someone else was there. In either case, he was probably "in the zone"—a state of mind many seek when exploring true wilderness by themselves, and a major goal for many in visiting the Church.

I explored areas that I had hunted forty and fifty years earlier. Honestly, I didn't hunt hard. I did glass the sagebrush slopes above a tributary that had held lots of deer in decades past, but didn't see any. Some of the old pack trails had been obliterated from forest fires and landslides and I found no new ones. At one point, I paused and peered down to where our base camp had always been set. A hint of a trail led down to the creek crossing and the grassy bench on the far side. I imagined the wall tent and a wisp of smoke, and then the slight clang of a bell around a donkey's neck followed by a whimper and then a full bray. The donkeys always greeted me when I returned to camp at the end of the day. Overcome by a bit of melancholy, and with a flood of memories, I moved by the site and studied the high mountain ridges and then the sky, giving thanks to God for the special place and His allowing me to visit it one more time.

RECIPES AFTER SUCCESS

Tons of quality meat was packed out of the backcountry of Idaho by my family and friends over the years. To my knowledge, we never lost any of it, and that was often a challenge. The weather could be hot, and when an animal was taken, it was a minimum of five days before the meat would reach our freezer back home. My Dad was all about meat care in the field, but was strange in that he didn't condone eating any while we were still in camp. Oh, for fresh deer tenderloin (rather than canned raviolis) I would plea, but he would have none of it. One thing we did eat plenty of in camp was Franklin's, or spruce grouse, aka "fool hens." Many were taken with arrows and blunts, some with just stones, and one as a gift from a goshawk than killed the bird in front of me and then abandoned it. The plentiful grouse supplemented many an otherwise mundane meal by adding to, or replacing, canned meat in a pasta dish. But my favorite way to eat them was to slice the meat thin, cook it in hot oil and salt for a minute or two in a skillet, and add to mashed potatoes.

I could share other backcountry recipes, but instead thought I would add a few suggestions for **further reading** about the Church. Here are a few of my favorites:

COUGAR DAVE – Mountain Man of Idaho 1855–1936
by Pat Cary Peek (Ninebark Publications, 2004; ISBN: 0-9753335-O-X).

The Middle Fork & The Sheepeater War by Johnny Carrey & Cort Conley (Backeddy Books, 1980; ISBN: 0-9603566-0-6).

Hanging and Rattling – Autobiography of W.E, "Ed" James as told to Dulcimer Nielsen (The Caxton Printers, LTD, 1979; ISBN: 0-87004-264-5).

7003 Days – 21 years in the Frank Church River of No Return Wilderness by Jim Akenson with Holly Akenson (*Caxton Press, 2016; ISBN: 978-087004-601-8*).

CHAPTER FIFTEEN

THE SETTING SUN

I guess there comes a time in many bowhunters' lives when they realize they have more hunts behind them than in front. It's a natural progression of things. Muscles weaken and joints ache, hearing fades, and stories seem to be more about the good old days than some planned new adventure. Then too, trophy rooms may be full and families smaller—homes may be downsized and the annual need to fill the freezer can diminish. I have reached that point in life. I have sold my heavier bows (though I have stowed a couple away that just have too many memories). I took most my big game trophies to an auction house before moving into a small home back in Alaska—to be closer to children and grandchildren. And I have become more selective in which hunts I undertake, focusing more and more on the experience and less and less on the probability of success. The many years of accumulated taxidermy work all saw significant time on a wall somewhere, allowing for memories to be relived every time I'd glance at them, but I saw little purpose keeping them in crates in storage after downsizing. Rather than bringing sadness, I found a bit of contentment in parting with all the mounts, skulls, and antlers. Though unknown buyers would not know the history of any particular trophy, they might still appreciate them for what they were. They must have wanted the stuff or wouldn't have bid on it, and in some small way, the animal might continue to be honored.

I practice less these days and realize my effective shooting distance is now little more than twenty yards, but I remain determined to maintain competency. Rather than going out for a day of practice, I'll shoot five or six times and put the bow down. Using weights to maintain strength is necessary, but equally important is regular stretching exercises. A good routine with simple resistance bands can pay off in the long run. Currently I am using the "Tyler twist" to treat a nasty case of lateral epicondylitis (tennis elbow) along with over and behind the back stretching exercises for my shoulders. Of course, maintaining cardio training will help with climbing the hills, and much of our lives may be improved if we keep our weight down and activity level up. I remember well what it was like to pack my gear and head to the hills for two-weeks of hunting without much thought of physical preparation, but those days are gone. The good news is I can still do most everything— some just takes longer, and some I choose not to do.

Looking back too, it doesn't take much memory to see the trend of reduced hunting opportunity in many places. While some small game hunting and hunting for deer and turkey in some states has kept pace with demand, many, if not most, hunting opportunities seem to be shrinking. This is particularly true for less common species and for nonresident hunters, and since everyone is a nonresident somewhere, the subject deserves some mention.

A number of court cases have reviewed challenges by nonresidents who cite unfair treatment. This comes most often from concern over far fewer tags and far higher fees for nonresident versus resident hunters, but also can come from other restrictions, like the requirement in Wyoming for nonresident hunters to hire a guide (or hunt with a resident) if they are in congressionally designated wilderness areas. This particularly irks some folks because all such areas are in federal ownership (and therefore all U.S. citizens should seemingly have equal use). No matter. To date, all such challenges have ultimately been resolved in favor of the states. Suffice it to say that the situation is not likely to improve. Resident hunters are being squeezed out of many of their traditional areas and voice their concern to sympathetic legislatures and wildlife commissions. While there are more and more people in the country—many of whom desire to pursue outdoor activities—there isn't any more land being made, and even with habitat improvement and increased access programs, opportunities for nonresidents are likely to continue to diminish. As such, if one wants to stay in the game, you have to learn to play it. It takes time and money. You should complete extensive research on every species you might be interested in pursuing, even if it could be a decade or more away before actually attempting to hunt. Building preference and bonus points for multiple species and in multiple states is simply the only way most hunters will ever have better than average opportunities to affordably pursue moose, goat, and sheep, and increasingly so, mule deer, elk, and pronghorn. Even with the best planning, however, states can and do change the rules. This recently happened in Wyoming after the legislature listened to resident hunter concerns and drastically reduced the number of permits nonresident hunters could get for moose and sheep. With nearly thirty bighorn sheep points accumulated, I got slammed by the change, having gone from only a year or two to wait for a tag, to the real likelihood of never drawing. Fortunately for me, I foresaw the likely change a year out and used my accumulated points to draw a moose tag while I still could, albeit for a lesser quality unit that I had hoped.

WYOMING MOOSE

Shiras moose are a subspecies of moose found in Montana, Colorado, Wyoming, Idaho, Utah, and Washington—with a few here and there in some adjacent states as well. They are known to be smaller than their northern cousins, both in body and antler size, but still are extremely large animals. They inhabit country from farmland to high wilderness crags to lowland sagebrush, but are most abundant in riparian zones and in young hardwood forests. To find them, look for their favorite foods: willow, young aspen or birch, and aquatic vegetation. I had hunted moose in Alaska extensively and for years didn't give the Shiras subspecies much thought. That changed as I started building preference points for other species and decided to build up moose points too, just in case I ever changed my mind. As the years passed, and the number of points grew, I did change my mind and was glad that I had started investing the many years before.

When the draw was completed, and my permit was in the mail, I wasn't really surprised that I had drawn. Based on previous years data, I was almost certain to draw the unit I had applied for. But with tag in hand, the preparation and planning began in earnest. I did all the usual stuff—started the physical training, ordered maps, and cleared the calendar with my wife—but I had another concern. I wanted to take my Shiras moose with traditional archery tackle and I frankly didn't know whether I could be ready to shoot a heavy enough set up to do the job well. I read a story about a bowhunter facing similar concerns that opted to use a traditional bow in the forty-pound range. He took a fine bull successfully, but I didn't know the circumstances, and my experiences with lighter bows on big game had been mixed. While a generality, I had found that an arrow from a forty-pound bow would likely penetrate six to ten inches on a deer; with fifty-pounds, more like ten inches to a complete pass through, and with sixty-pounds, almost always a complete pass through, even if ribs were broken in the process. Moose are a whole lot bigger than deer. I set a goal to use a recurve that pulled in the mid-fifties, heavy arrows, a slender broadhead, and I planned to get close, very close.

A good friend from church, Rocky Wardle, agreed to join me on the Wyoming hunt. Knowing that I would likely draw the moose tag, we pooled our preference points for elk and applied for them on a party application. Wyoming allows hunters for many species (including deer, elk, and moose) to hunt with archery tackle prior to the regular firearm season. An archery license is required, but it is a cheap addition to the nonresident tag fees, and allows archers considerable time in the field before the guns come out. Wyoming does allow crossbows to be used under their archery rules. Rocky, not being a bowhunter, borrowed a quality crossbow and practiced with it a great deal before the trip. Some might think that pairing up with a crossbow hunter might lead to conflict; however, just like sharing your camp with both traditional bowhunters and those with compound bows, the weapon does not make the hunter. Honesty, a willingness to share the work, having a sense of humor, being safety conscious and ethical, are attributes I look for in choosing hunting partners, and Rocky excelled in all of them. Besides, while his weapon was capable of shooting considerable distance, Rocky did not use it that way. His planned and practice shots were in the same basic range as mine. I want to mention here that I am not a big fan of crossbows, but my only real concern is with their potential wide use in archery seasons. I believe that this could ultimately be bad for hunting and therefore conservation. This belief allows that there is no significant harm in allowing crossbows to be used in "any weapon" hunts, and little harm for isolated uses here and there—for short specific seasons or for use by those who have severe disabilities. The harm, I believe, could come with their widespread use that could significantly increase harvest within shorter time periods, leading to fewer tags and/or shorter seasons. This could result in less opportunity and less incentive to hunt. Simply put, I expect far fewer folks would participate in the hunting sports if they had to trade a several week-long season for a weekend or two, or had to wait several years in between hunts, and anything that might contribute to this is something I would likely oppose. I realize that the same equation is already in play comparing traditional archery equipment with modern compounds. It can come into play too for muzzleloading equipment and even high-powered rifles—variability exists with most categories of weapons that impact success, and therefore, the potential opportunity offered. These are complex issues for wildlife managers to address. We all have our preferences, and managers must try to be fair and recognize everyone's personal choices the best they can. In doing so, I hope they continue to recognize that offering limited range weapon hunts can create significantly more opportunity for hunters to be afield, and that is a good thing, not only for traditional bowhunters but also for all who support maintaining hunting and its contributions to conservation.

Weapon choices may be important,
but they do not make the hunter.

The plan for Rocky and I was to arrive a few days before the season to scout several areas, to focus on moose first, and if successful, switch over to elk, but as the seasons would be open at the same time, if elk entered the picture while searching for moose, we would shift gears accordingly. We drove separate vehicles so that we would have a super comfortable camp, and in case one of us needed to return to Oregon early with meat or for other reasons.

The first couple of days we walked a little, drove a lot, and glassed for hours. We saw a few deer, one small bull elk, a bear, and a cow moose. We moved camp to a drainage to the north and started anew. We heard several bull elk bugle the first morning and spooked a couple more; we also spotted a half-dozen moose, including several bulls. We had found the place we would concentrate and began to hunt in earnest. On the third morning of serious hunting, Rocky dropped me off in the dark several miles from camp, and I planned to parallel the road while hunting back. I climbed the hill slowly until it was light enough to see and then sped up a bit, trying to cover the country quickly until I found fresh sign. Moose are often in isolated spots across the landscape and may stay in the same general area if they have everything they need (food, water, and cover) and if they remain undisturbed. And they leave lots of sign in such places. Within the first hour of light, I came to a thick grove of young hardwoods in a recent burn. In the middle of it was a series of springs and boggy areas and moose sign was everywhere. The tracks and dropping were large—I assumed left by a bull. I slowed down to full stealth mode and scanned the area ahead. Nothing. I crept on, soon leaving the boggy area and entering an open forest. It wasn't long however until I came to another spring area surrounded by grass and willows. Fresh moose sign saturated this area too, but I saw no animals. I kept moving forward and leaned under some alders to avoid catching my daypack and saw two large brown forms ahead. They were moose, both bulls, but they had seen my movement too. I slowly sat down and took a breath. The bulls stood side by side for a few minutes and then turned and ran slowly away. I checked the wind. It was still good. They hadn't smelled me. Perhaps they weren't too spooked and wouldn't go far? I waited twenty minutes and then slowly followed. There were enough fresh moose tracks that I couldn't tell whether I was really on their trail or not, so I just went where I thought a moose might go. About when I thought I would never see them again, I did. They had separated, now about 150 yards from each other, and both were actively feeding. I focused on the closer bull on my downhill side. When he walked, I walked. I followed for nearly a half hour, closing the distance steadily. When the bull fed into a thick brush patch over a slight rise ahead, I quickly closed most of the distance between us and then snuck forward for a peek, arrow ready. The bull was directly ahead, in range, and unaware of my presence, but it was too thick for a shot. I had to wait. He then started to walk briskly across a small opening. I saw a clear shooting lane ahead and swung on the bull while drawing back. Conscious of the size of the animal and my bow's limits, I paused for an instant to ensure I had maximum draw, and then released. The slight delay was my excuse for hitting the bull a little farther back than intended, though the shot was still forward of the paunch and looked good. Penetration was less than hoped for too, but the arrow was in solid. It would be fine I was sure—at least as sure as I could be, but there is often a bit of anxiety and I admit I felt some. I waited for the moose to move out of sight. It ran upon being hit, but then stopped, ran again, stopped, and then disappeared through distant trees. I followed its trail for sixty yards or so and found abundant dark blood first—evidence of a liver hit—followed by bright red frothy blood. The arrow had apparently struck the liver and one lung. I knew this was a fatal hit, but it was still early and the morning was cool. I decided to leave the trail and come back in a few hours with my partner.

Back at camp, Rocky and I discussed how long we should wait before returning to where I had shot the bull. We agreed that several more hours might be ideal, but that we didn't know how long it might take to find the animal, and once recovered, we would have a lot of work to do, and we would prefer to complete it during daylight hours. We geared up and returned to the spot I had stopped following the blood trail. It was easy to pick up again and easy to follow. It led to the bull bedded in a willow patch, easy to see but still alive. After a follow-up shot, the work began. We gutted, skinned, and quartered the animal and backpacked some and drug the rest of the meat on a tarp down to the dirt road below. We finished the work at last light, and I pulled my headlamp out of my fanny pack and sipped from my water bottle as Rocky went for the truck. It had been a long but good day.

We hung the meat for a couple of days and then took it to a cooler in the closest town to keep the quarters and boned meat frozen until we were ready to go home. Another consideration for many out-of-state hunters these days, are the special requirements for transporting harvested deer, elk, and moose home because of the potential of spreading chronic wasting disease (CWD). The disease is fatal to ungulates, is becoming widespread, and is a major concern for hunters and game managers. Because CWD concentrates in the brain and spinal fluid of animals, most states now have requirements that require all flesh to be completely removed and the boiling of skulls before transporting them into their state. Wyoming went a step further and required this be done before transporting the game out of the management unit it was taken. I had planned for this and brought the necessary equipment; however, the front part of the moose skull had to be sawed off so everything would fit in the galvanized basin I had brought, and the volume of water needed to cover the skull barely would come to a boil even with the two propane stoves I used. The effort took all day, but it was also a day I was visited by a game warden in camp. He let me know how much he appreciated the effort. I gathered that not everyone was strictly following the new CWD rules.

Wyoming moose.

With the moose secured, we switched gears to elk. We got close several times in coming days, but no arrows were released. One morning, we were working a herd that had two very vocal satellite bulls and a large overly protective herd bull. All the boys were talking and running about. They were responding well to our cow calling when we also called up another hunter who started aggressively cow-calling too. Even though Rocky was well armed with his crossbow, and could have easily taken a shot, he was looking for something under thirty yards. The other hunter shot one of the approaching bulls with his compound at about sixty yards. We watched it all unfold, waited until the bull was down, and then went over to congratulate the hunter. He was from out-of-state too, and was obviously pleased. We didn't burst his bubble. Instead, I took his photo for him with his I-phone and left him to his work. The bull didn't belong to us. The other hunter had just as much right to take it as we did. Still, as I looked at his modern bow and its expensive sighting system, the 10-mm pistol on his belt, Garmin InReach hanging from his pack, rangefinder binoculars around his neck, and what had to be nearly $1,000 worth of camo, I thought, "bowhunting has changed." This young fellow had driven his side-by-side ATV from his camp over thirty miles away in the dark, listening for elk here and there along the way. Upon hearing some, he began his pursuit and wasn't dissuaded by the fact that other hunters were already closely pursuing the animals. He used high-tech equipment to take the animal, and there was little doubt that the culmination of it all was how he defined success. But who was I to judge? I had no right. And when I reflect on the series of events of that morning, and other similar situations that I have witnessed in recent years, I sometimes will share that at least there is a next generation bowhunting—at least the sport is being perpetuated. But then again, I may wonder if it really is the same sport that I found so appealing so many years ago. But it is what we make it. We choose how we will hunt, what equipment we will use, and how we will treat others. In such a way, bowhunting hasn't really changed much at all. It is a sport that individuals can decide how they wish to participate—an ancient sport and a modern one—a sport for kings and peasants—my chosen sport.

A CONSERVATION CONVERSATION

Many in society may not agree that hunting is a conservation tool. It can seem counterintuitive that killing animals somehow can benefit them too. Of course, I am speaking about the take of individual animals and with potential benefit to populations. As an aging wildlife biologist this idea probably resonates with me better than with many others— many who probably come from more of an urban setting, and with a higher concern for animal welfare than maybe those from my generation. I don't blame Disney or other media. The material they produce is popular because it appeals to a large audience. They aren't brainwashing anyone. I think there is a natural empathy for other living creatures held by most humans, but that it can also be swayed to more extremes when nurtured in isolation from the entirety of nature. All life ends in death and the vast majority of death occurs in nature so that other creatures can live. I can remember chickens having their heads removed with a hatchet, soon to enter scalding water and being plucked, dressed, and cut into frying pieces. I remember all of the sights, sounds, and smells of this operation. I also remember the sights, sounds, and smells of the birds hours later as they sizzled in Crisco in a cast iron skillet. I can remember the taste too! Growing up harvesting your own meat, whether wild or farm-raised, may create a different perspective about hunting over growing up simply removing the cellophane wrapper from what you have purchased. But in either case, empathy for wildlife is important. Animals should not be killed merely for fun, and whenever they are taken, it should be done as humanely as possible. That does not rule out the use of traditional archery equipment for the task. Done ethically, with practice and restraint, taking animals with a bow can be just as humane, if not more so, than with a high-powered rifle. I have relayed a few examples in stories I have shared where clean kills did not immediately result after an arrow struck. If you hunt long enough, this will happen, regardless of the weapon used. Ethical hunters will do everything in their power to minimize suffering and loss of their prey. If they don't, nonhunters may exercise their democratic rights to limit hunting further. I say "nonhunters" rather than anti-hunters. The later will always try to eliminate hunting in all of its forms, but nonhunters comprise the bulk of U.S. voters—people who don't hunt but aren't necessarily against it. As the majority, nonhunters may easily decide the fate of hunting. Polls seem to continue to demonstrate that nonhunters in the United States will support hunting as long as the animals are used for food and when it is conducted safely and humanely.

I mentioned earlier of my concern for increasingly efficient weaponry that could result in less hunting opportunity and there-fore less hunters. I suggested that this could ultimately be bad for conservation, but I didn't fully explain why. Certainly, hunters are not the only people who care about wildlife, or support beneficial wildlife conservation initiatives. But they continue to be the group that pays for most wildlife management in this country. They do so through license fees; excise taxes on firearms, archery equipment, and ammunition; and through memberships and donations to con-servation organizations. Without such contributions, there would be very little done for habitat improvement, or new habitat acquisition. Wildlife research would be limited and wildlife reintroductions and transplants would nearly cease. There would be impacts to dedicated law enforcement, special wildlife feeding programs, disease control, and population monitoring. Elsewhere in the world, if hunting was stopped, the economic incentive for maintaining sustainable popu-lations of game would be over-shadowed by desires for more agri-cultural land and less competition with, and risk from, many wildlife species. Too, if people hunger, wildlife has to have more value to them than something just intrinsic. They will eat them or replace them with something they can eat.

There are many conservation issues of concern today. Well-managed hunting isn't one of them. Climate change stands tall over any other issue in the long run, and whether you buy into the claimed cause or proposed cures, changes are occurring and managers are struggling to keep up. When the climate changes, so does the land-scape—some animals may benefit from the change and others not. Overall, rapid change is predicted to result in increased extinction rates. This, along with a growing human population and its unstoppable consumption of land and natural resources, foretells of greater challenges ahead for conservationists. Hunters, all hunters, should be informed participants in shaping the social/biological/political future of our country. They have a lot to lose in upcoming decisions, and they have a lot to offer in helping to shape them.

A FULL QUIVER

As I have aged, I often think more pleasure can be gained from giving than taking—giving back to the sport that created so much joy during younger years. This can be done in a variety of ways, but mentoring youth may be one of the most rewarding. I know I would have likely never been introduced to archery in the way I was without the care and guidance I received from Dick Bonney. Dick was a prolific writer as well as teacher, mentor, and advocate. In the last article that Dick wrote he said, "I will not be here forever, and I am trying to perfect a teaching core that will endure long after I have moved on to the Happy Hunting Grounds." Through years of dedicated effort, I believe Dick achieved his desired goal and far more. I suspect many other bowhunters can point to similar situations and personal histories—having an individual or group of people that helped offer advice, supplied equipment if needed, provided occasional transportation, and created an atmosphere of fun.

Bowhunting opportunities for future generations may well be determined by the collective actions of hunters now.

Aging bowhunters can find enjoyment later in life by supporting a local 4-H or other archery club, donating old equipment, and/ or taking a young person hunting. I have known a few old codgers who resist helping young bowhunters join their ranks. They may believe the woods are already too crowded so why help increase the competition. Sadly, such folks may breathe their last while harboring bits of anger and frustration rather than with a smile on their face as they remember witnessing the joys of youngsters as they get bit by the traditional bowhunting bug. It is these people that give back who will more likely leave this life in contentment—with countless fond memories of campfires with family and friends, of wild places and trophies taken—and those that got away, and with the knowledge that the tradition is being passed on—to provide the next generation the same invaluable experiences. It is with a compliment of such memories that one may best leave this life—with a proverbial full quiver.